GLAD TIDINGS OF STRUGGLE AND STRIFE

Tynnwyd o'r stoc
Withdrawn

A HISTORY OF PROTEST CHRISTMAS CARDS

LLEW AND PAM SMITH

Foreword by KEN LIVINGSTONE

FONTHILL

Fonthill Media Limited

Fonthill Media LLC

www.fonthillmedia.com

office@fonthillmedia.com

First published in the United Kingdom 2012

British Library Cataloguing in Publication Data:
A catalogue record for this book is available from the British Library

ISBN 978-1-78155-185-1 (print)

ISBN 978-1-78155-200-1 (e-book)

Typeset in 9.5pt on 13pt Sabon

Printed and bound in England

Connect with us

 facebook.com/fonthillmedia  twitter.com/fonthillmedia

Contents

Acknowledgements

To my late wife, Pam, who spent many hours, over many years, helping to build this collection, and contributed to the research and writing for this book.

To many fine writers, particularly: James Cameron, Noam Chomsky, Michael and Paul Foot, John Pilger, Bertrand Russell and the many correspondents to the Letters Columns of various newspapers, whose ideas we have drawn upon.

The artists and publishers of the cards who have kindly allowed us to use their work and who had the skill and the forethought to record these important events – especially: Trudy Begg, Steve Bell, Maggie Guillon, Alan Hardman, Paul Morton, Stuart Ritchie, Martin Rowson and Steve Smith.

To those comrades and friends, who kindly shared their collections with us – especially the late Sid Brown, the late Alex Falconer, Peter Moloney, Leeds Postcards and *The Morning Star*.

Also to Jeanne Smith, Eleanor Smith, Simon Smith and Mary Bradley for their help and commitment to this project.

Last but by no means least, those who had the courage to act and the wit to see that action was necessary.

The authors' royalties from the sale of this book will be donated to the People's History Museum, Manchester.

Preface

Sadly, my wife Pam, who was jointly responsible for the collection of Christmas cards and the compilation of this book, died before it was completed. Any shortcomings in the final version are therefore mine. We did not attempt to write a comprehensive history of government policy, or of protest, but merely, of those which became the subject of Christmas cards, from the mid-nineteenth century to the present day. Some may have been produced, which our research failed to uncover. The cards included in this book only represent a small part of our total collection, but hopefully, those selected provide an insight into our people's history.

In attempting to write this aspect of history, we faced a number of other difficulties, including tracing the individual or organisation responsible for producing these cards (any help in this regard would be appreciated). It has also been difficult to identify the dates they were published and linked to this, the government they were referring to. This is further complicated when certain issues and policies are relevant to more than one government and when their responses to them are almost identical. An example of this would be New Labour, Liberal Democrats and the Tories, who, while having different names, still shared some similar beliefs on issues such as privatisation. Christmas cards produced in different periods may also have identical designs, as with the CND symbol and the dove of peace.

Also, because there are a very limited number of 'political' Christmas cards produced in the earlier periods, we have included the date of the struggle in examples where the relevant cards may have been produced many years after the event.

For a number of reasons, the book mainly concentrates on policies, events and protests within the United Kingdom, other than those that affect us while happening beyond our borders.

The sentiments expressed and conclusions reached are unashamedly those of two socialists, my late wife Pam and myself. However, there are some cards which do not necessarily represent our personal views, but as they are an important part of our history they have been included.

As activists, we had the privilege of campaigning alongside many truly remarkable 'rebels' and 'revolutionaries', most of whom never received a mention in our history books, but nevertheless, we are still indebted to them.

There are a few cards included, which, strictly speaking, are not Christmas cards; they were produced at that time of the year, but they make no reference to the celebration because of the secular nature of the organisation responsible for their production. Finally, we contend that like the banners and placards we have waved, the leaflets we have distributed and the protest songs we have sung, many of these Christmas cards also deserve a proud place as a means of 'getting our message over'. They are an important part of our rich history.

Foreword

Llew and Pam Smith had the original idea of looking at the history of protest through the Christmas card.

This unexpected medium serves as a guide to how struggles for a fairer and more just society have unfolded. The images assembled for this collection move through the stages of that history, from the early days of the Labour movement to the creation of the Labour Party and on to the achievements and limitations of Government.

A consistent theme has also been the campaign for peace, from the horror of the First World War to the anti-nuclear weapons movement. The call for a world without war shown here chimes with the message of Christmas.

This is a welcome and often surprising collection that adds to our understanding of how people have talked about their values and hopes for the future at a time of the year that encourages reflection and goodwill.

Ken Livingstone

The Way Ahead

'It is through disobedience that progress is made.' – *Oscar Wilde*

'Our lives begin to end the day we become silent about things that matter.' – *Martin Luther King Jr*

'For working class movements, history has always been a weapon, the best at their disposal, to sustain their pride, their refusal to be broken by exploitation, their fighting solidarity, their shared aspirations.' – *Michael Foot*

'What matters to me is the response from below, from the people at the bottom of the pile. If they don't respond, history becomes slack and even dull. When they do respond, especially when they revolt, history comes to life.' – *Paul Foot*

'We have it in our power to begin the world over again.' – *Tom Paine*

'I am not prepared to forget and forgive the wrongs done to my people. We need twenty years of power to transfer the citadels of capitalism from the hands of a few people to the control of the nation. Only after twenty years can we afford to be polite. Then maybe I won't have enough energy to be rude, but while we have the energy, let us be rude to the right people.' – *Aneurin Bevan*

'Don't say "um" or "erm". Three simple words: We; need; change.' – *Written on a wall within the Royal College of Art (2012)*

CHAPTER 1

The Christmas Card, Born in Times of Struggle

'An old and unending worldwide company, the men and women of conscience. Some are as famous as Tom Paine ... some are unknown as a tiny group calling itself Grandmothers Against the Bomb ... who have gone cheerfully to jail for their protests. There have always been such people and always will be. If they win, it is slowly; but they never entirely lose. To my mind, they are the blessed proof of the dignity of man.'[1]

– Martha Gellhorn

Be prepared, for this is not a history of the humble Christmas card with messages described by one of their early designers as 'unconsidered trifles'[2], but a record of much of the political, industrial and social turmoil since the mid-nineteenth century. Many of these cards portray the words and deeds of those who, in the face of injustice, refused to remain silent and accept that nothing could be done. Such individuals are almost invariably seen as a threat to the established order and are often described as 'rebels' or 'revolutionaries'. However, many have helped to mould our history and are responsible for countless advances we have made; we have been taught too often to associate progress solely with kings, queens, generals and landowners.

The Christmas card, with the themes of peace, goodwill, justice and hope, was seen as an appropriate medium by the 'rebels' to project what they considered as similar aspirations.

If the Christmas card had appeared in earlier times, some may have portrayed the events surrounding the hostility towards the landlords in the fourteenth century; the supporters of the Peasants' Revolt, the Levellers and the Diggers of the seventeenth century; the Paineite Revolt in the eighteenth century; and the Tolpuddle Martyrs, Rebecca Riots of the nineteenth century.

Indeed, how some of these may have been portrayed can be seen by a twentieth-century Christmas card, using the traditional drawing of 'when Adam Delved and Eve Span who was then the Gentleman'. The image and words had been used in the fourteenth century to highlight injustice and opposition to the landlords. According to Froissart, John Ball turned this conventional statement on Christian humility into a radical call for social equality. 'He tried to prove ... that from the beginning all men were created equal by nature and that servitude had been introduced by the unjust and evil oppression of men against the will of God....'[3] The card also includes the sentiments expressed by John Ball who wrote, '... matters will not go well in England till all things be made common; when there shall be neither serfs nor lords; when the lords shall be no more masters than ourselves.'

Left: From a pen and ink drawing by Edward Burne-Jones. Printed by Marx Memorial Library, 37a Clerkenwell Green, London EC18 0DU.

Below: 'The first real Christmas card, designed by J. C. Horsley in 1843 at the suggestion and request of his friend, Henry Cole.' Published at Summerlys Home Treasury Office, 12 Old Bond Street, London.

The first real Christmas card, designed by J. C. Horsley in 1843 at the suggestion and request of his friend, Henry Cole. The photograph shows a particularly interesting copy: it is the one sent to Henry Cole by the artist who signed the card by a small caricature of himself with palette and brushes. The date is clearly "Xmasse, 1843".

> The coming hope — the future day,
>
> When wrong to right shall bow,
>
> And but a little courage, man!
>
> To make that future — now!
>
> **ERNEST JONES**
> *Chartist Poet, 1852*

Poem by Ernest Jones,
Chartist poet, 1852.

Yet the events that followed those of earlier centuries have resulted in an equally rich history, and many of these events were recorded in Christmas cards.

Coinciding with many of the nineteenth-century struggles was the publication of the first Christmas card in 1843, designed by J. C. Horsley (the postage from sending the cards, would, it was claimed, help to keep taxes down). The message on the card was an example of what one of the early designers described as 'unconsidered trifles', with the words 'A Merry Christmas and a Happy New Year'.[4]

Yet one can argue that the visual image, as opposed to the words, was more than an 'unconsidered trifle'; it is reflective of the class-based nature of society at that time. Central to the picture is a 'happy' and obviously affluent Victorian family, sharing a fine bottle of wine. Yet at both ends of the picture are some of the victims of that system, reflecting that class divide, with the poor shown to be dependent on, among other things, charity for their food and clothing.

The 'master', as portrayed in this Christmas card, would almost certainly have become increasingly concerned with the challenging of the status quo and the increased militancy of the lower classes in the years surrounding the publication of this card.

This militancy was to take many different forms, one being the growth of the Chartist movement, which was to become three million strong and increasingly armed. Like the Levellers of the seventeenth century, the Chartists were seen as dangerous revolutionaries; they demanded the vote, which the 'masters' feared would be used to take away their wealth. If this had been successful, then the first Christmas card may have required a role reversal, with the 'masters' being forced to accept the crumbs.

A Christmas card produced in recent years includes verse written by one of these Chartist leaders, Ernest Jones, who was imprisoned in the most horrendous conditions. It includes the sentiments which many of the masters feared: 'The coming hope – the future day, when wrong to right shall bow, and but a little courage, man! To make that future – now!'

Sadly, the revolutionary nature of their movement subsided and the vote was not achieved for a number of years; the position of the masters remained intact.

In the nineteenth century poverty continued, as did militancy, taking many forms to obtain better wages, a shorter working week and improved working and living conditions. The employers often responded with lock outs as a weapon to smash trade societies.

The Mechanics Institute, birthplace of the TUC, 1868. 103 Princess Street, Manchester M1 6DD.

Simultaneously, there were also fears that the Royal Commission of Inquiry would come down in favour of returning to the laws of 1821, when trade unions were made illegal.

Faced by a wide range of attacks, trade unions were increasingly vulnerable and lacked a national body to speak on their behalf. The call went out, 'why not have a congress of our own?' In 1868 the call was met at the Mechanics Institute in Manchester, with the First Trades Union Congress.

One delegate, A. W. Bailey, addressing that first Congress, highlighted the feeling of exploitation and the unfairness of the system, declaring that : '... the capitalist was rich , the labourer poor; the capitalist strong, sometimes arrogant and oppressive; the labourer weak, submissive and defenceless.... An individual working man could not drive a just and equitable bargain with the capitalists under such conditions. The power of combination was only just sufficient to counteract the power the capitalist possessed....'[5]

In more recent years, a Christmas card was produced to recognise and celebrate that Congress and the Institute of 1868.

In the latter part of the nineteenth century, the theme and hopes of the Congress were reflected by the artist Walter Crane in some of the earliest political and socialist Christmas cards. The cards, while still carrying the traditional greetings of 'Merry Christmas and a Happy New Year were nevertheless followed by '... with good luck to Labour, hand, heart and brain, stick fast to your banner, stand solid, not veer, till the cause of the workers renews earth again.... The Cause of Labour is the Hope of the World.'

Another of Walter Crane's Christmas cards demands, 'Work for all – Art for all.'

Above left and right: Designed by the socialist painter Walter Crane (1845-1915). Hand tinted by Alex Corina. Published by the Labour Party, 150 Walworth Road, London SE17 1JT. Leeds Postcards, PO Box 84, Leeds LS1 4HU.

David Gerard, an authority on Crane, stated that the latter's reading of Shelley and Liberal thinkers like J. S. Mill had aroused his creativity and his artist's enthusiasm for the liberation of the imaginative potential in every person. This led him 'to ponder the nature of society in which such potential could be given full expression. It surely must be a society based on equality and freedom from poverty and exploitation.'[6]

Gerard goes on to remind us that, 'Henceforth his fondness for allegory and symbolism would be transferred from the past to the present, translated into political messages: winged figures in flowing costume, one derived from myths, would be turned into powerful emblems of the struggle, designed to encourage not only revolutionary change, but a new consciousness that art can transform life....'[7]

Crane's work, as we have shown, is still popular today, especially within the Labour Movement, and his Christmas cards are frequently re-issued.

As the nineteenth century progressed, one of the other causes of rising concern for many 'masters' was the revolutionary ideas of Karl Marx. Among many other things, Marx explained how the class nature of society benefitted those with excessive wealth at the expense of those who produced the wealth – labour. This Christmas card was produced in 1987, showing his gravestone of 1883.

During the latter part of the nineteenth century, Christmas cards began to appear portraying other political events, including those produced after the massive demonstration in Trafalgar Square on 13 November 1887 which came to be known as 'Bloody Sunday'.

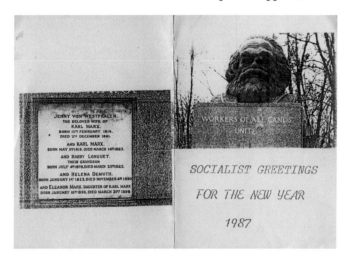

Left: Tomb of Karl Marx; artist unknown.

Below: Artist E. G. 'Fight at the Bottom of Parliament Street.'

This Christmas card, although not resembling typical cards, was seemingly sold in large numbers and reflected 'the fight at the bottom of Parliament Street.'

The demonstration had been called and went ahead, in defiance of a government ban. The historian, Clive Bloom, explained the ban, which resulted from a decision taken by Sir Charles Warren, Commissioner of the Metropolitan Police, that 'no Public Meetings will be allowed to assemble in Trafalgar Square, nor will speeches be allowed to be delivered therein.'[8] The 'notice outraged the left, who saw the Square as a prime venue [in a rapidly shrinking pool] for their protests. Freedom of speech was clearly threatened as was the ancient right of people to meet and consult. The occasion of Warren's notice, a ban on a proposed meeting on behalf of William O'Brien, an imprisoned Irish Home Rule advocate, was now to be made into a protest over the gagging of freedom of speech and freedom of assembly.'[9]

Above right: Angus Thomas copyright. 'Ode to the Specials.'

Right: 'The Federated Postmen of Sheffield.' W. A. Rose & Co. Spear Street, Oldham Street, Manchester.

Below: From the collection at the Working Class Movement Library, Salford.

In the sweet days of yore, when Divinity rode
On His mission of Love, an ass He bestrode.

But woe for the change! It now takes, alas,

Two men and two horses to carry an ass.

The Trustees and Staff of the
Working Class Movement Library

Thank you for
all your support over
the past year

The demonstrators were met and savagely beaten at Trafalgar Square by an estimated 2,000 police, many of them on horses, together with 'specials' and 400 troops. Many demonstrators were severely injured and two died. In addition, many arrests were made; John Burn and Cunninghame Green were imprisoned for six weeks.

An Inquiry was held following the demonstration and one would have hoped – naïvely – that the savagery of the police, the 'specials' and the army would have dominated it. Instead, the main conclusion reached was that the truncheons should be made stronger and easier to carry. Considering the number of injuries and deaths, the truncheon seemed more than adequate.

The Times, true to their class instincts, saw the events in a totally different light, reporting that, '... It was no enthusiasm for free speech ... and no honest purpose that animated those howling toughs. It was a simple love of disorder, hope of plunder.'[10]

Although subject to acts of savagery, the demonstrators took to the streets a few days later with a public meeting and once again met with a similarly violent outcome, with many injured and another killed.

A Christmas card glorifying the violence inflicted by the police 'specials' was produced by one of them, Angus Thomas. The only artistry included in this card was a truncheon, used by the police 'specials' and others, to violently attack the demonstrators, with tragic results. The words reflect the glorification of the violence by the 'specials'.

A far more peaceful protest came in 1893, with the Federated Postmen of Sheffield presenting their petition to the government, which included a number of demands for improved 'wages, hours, holidays and procedures for promotion'. The demands were drafted in times of anti-trade unionism and when those involved were easily victimised.

Gordon A. Forsyth. Published by Independent Labour Party Centenary Celebration Trust.

'James Keir Hardie.' Artist unknown.

The petition was rejected, but the *Postman's Gazette* still concluded, 'Comrades ... stand firm! Education and self-discipline follow in the train of organisation, and to organise we must give our best.'[11]

On the subject of the privileged, one Christmas card hints at the growing class consciousness, comparing humble Jesus riding an 'ass', with what seems to be a member of the landed gentry, being described as an 'ass', as he was carried by a carriage, two men and two horses.

In 1893, the Independent Labour Party was formed by, among others, Keir Hardie. In the latter part of the twentieth century, a card portraying an Independent Labour Party Conference was used as the basis of a Christmas card celebrating the 100th anniversary of the birth of the party.

Towards the end of the twentieth century, a picture of Keir Hardie was used in a Christmas card in recognition of his role in the Labour Movement. Hardie put many radical issues before Parliament, often upsetting the establishment. With George Lansbury he opposed the Boer War at the end of the nineteenth century. This war was an example of British imperialism, demonstrating a willingness to plunder a country, killing tens of thousands of its people who had never posed a threat to the British, merely for private profits from the marketing of African gold and diamonds. In 1915, when Rosa Luxembourg wrote that 'profits are springing like weeds, from the seeds of the dead,'[12] she could also have been commenting on the Boer and many other wars.

Notes on Chapter 1

1. Martha Gellhorn, quoted in *Distant Voices* by John Pilger, 1992, explaining that Pilger was a part of that long and fine tradition.
2. Quoted in *The History of the Christmas Carol*, George Buday, Omnigraphics, 1992.
3. Edward Vallance, *A Radical History of Britain*, Little, Brown, 2009.
4. Quoted in *The History of the Christmas Carol*, George Buday, Omnigraphics 1992.
5. A. W. Bailey, quoted in *1868 Year of the Unions*, edited, with introduction and notes by Edmund Trow and Michael Katanka, Michael Katanka (Books) Ltd, London, 1968.
6. David Gerard, *Walter Crane and the Rhetoric of Art*, The Nine Elms Press.
7. David Gerard, *Walter Crane and the Rhetoric of Art*, The Nine Elms Press.
8. Clive Bloom, *Violent London*, Pan Books, 2004.
9. Clive Bloom, *Violent London*, Pan Books, 2004.
10. *The Times*, 14 November 1887.
11. *Postman's Gazette*, 1893.
12. Rosa Luxembourg, *Junius Pamphlet*, 1915.

CHAPTER 2

A New Century,
But Old Struggles Continue

'Agitators we have been and agitators we must remain if we are to be of use to Socialism.'[1]

– Keir Hardie

The twentieth century opened and continued where the nineteenth century had closed: with the Boer War; the militancy of many trade union struggles in response to falling wages; and the suffragettes demanding votes for women.

The Boer War was to end in 1902 with the winners being not so much a country, but a class and a system of imperialism, with the rewards of African gold and diamonds only for a few.

Meanwhile, trade union action became more militant. One of the trade union banners of the early part of this century was portrayed and reproduced in a recent Christmas card. The banner of the National Union of Railwaymen carries the demand for 'political' and 'industrial' action, to bring about the 'liberation of the working class.'

As for the Suffragettes, many of their grievances and struggles are highlighted in the Christmas cards of that period. One was a reminder to their 'brothers' who supported their struggles, that 'deeds not words, who would be free himself, must strike the first blow.'

Indeed, these deeds were often to lead to their imprisonment, which was seemingly welcomed by the designer of another card.

The suffragettes were, in reality, a number of groups, with differing opinions on important issues.

On the subject of industrial action by trade unionists, particularly the miners, Emmaline Pankhurst was of the opinion that they were 'paralysing the whole life of the community.'[2] Christabel Pankhurst demanded to know if the government proposed 'to make the organisation of strikes punishable by law.'[3] The demands emblazoned on the NUR banner – 'the liberation of the working class is the act of the workers themselves' – would not have received any support, nor those made by other unions, from either Emmaline or Christabel; they seemed to ignore, or did not care about the poverty of that period.

Yet for some suffragettes, any action was still acceptable, including the bombing of property in the pursuit of their cause. Indeed, in justifying attacks on property, Mrs Emmaline Pankhurst of the Women's Social and Political Union argued that '... there is something that governments care for, more than they care for human life and that is the security of property. Property to them is far more dear and tender than is human life and so it is through property that we shall strike the enemy ...'[4] This seems almost a Marxist analysis on the priority of property, a view which, in general, she would not share.

Above left: Rickmansworth Branch Banner (face) *c.* 1914 (photo: John Gorman Collection). Printed in England by Sandwell Printing Ltd and Published by NUR Publicity department.

Above right: Artist: Holloway, 'Who would be free.'

Right: 'Suffragette Imprisoned'. People's History Museum, Manchester.

Their differences were also highlighted in their attitude towards the First World War. Commenting on war, Adela Pankhurst writes:

> I didn't raise my son to be a soldier;
> I brought him up to be my pride and
> joy. Who dares to put a musket on his
> shoulder. To kill some other mother's
> darling boy.[5]

Emmaline Pankhurst had no sympathy with this kind of sentiment and instead demanded a suspension of militant activities, concentrating on supporting the war effort.

I have mainly concentrated on the Pankhursts' when referring to the suffragettes, because the divisions within that family, in many ways, reflected those in the wider women's movement.

With the end of the First World War, came the announcement that women over thirty years of age who fulfilled certain qualifications had been awarded the right to vote. A decade later, the age limit was reduced to twenty-one.

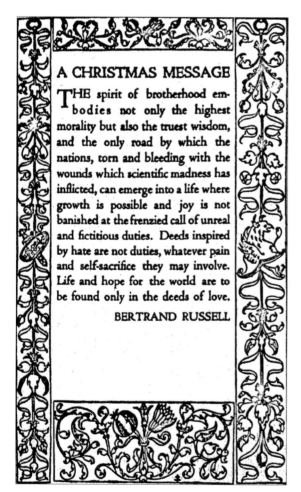

A CHRISTMAS MESSAGE

THE spirit of brotherhood embodies not only the highest morality but also the truest wisdom, and the only road by which the nations, torn and bleeding with the wounds which scientific madness has inflicted, can emerge into a life where growth is possible and joy is not banished at the frenzied call of unreal and fictitious duties. Deeds inspired by hate are not duties, whatever pain and self-sacrifice they may involve. Life and hope for the world are to be found only in the deeds of love.

BERTRAND RUSSELL

Bertrand Russell: 'A Christmas Message.'

WITH ALL GOOD WISHES
AT CHRISTMAS FOR THE
PEACE OF THE WORLD

THE WORLD THAT WE MUST seek is one in which the creative spirit is alive, in which life is full of joy and hope, based more upon the impulse to construct than upon the desire to retain what we possess. It must be a world in which affection has free play, in which love has destroyed the instinct for domination, and cruelty and envy have been dispelled by happiness. Such a world is possible; it waits only for men to wish to create it. The old world is passing away, burnt up in the fire of its own fierce passions; and from its ashes will spring a new and younger world, full of fresh hope, with the light of morning in its eyes.

BERTRAND RUSSELL

Above left and right: Percy F. Horton, from the Liddle Collection at Leeds University.

Below: Roy Richmond, from the Liddle Collection at Leeds University.

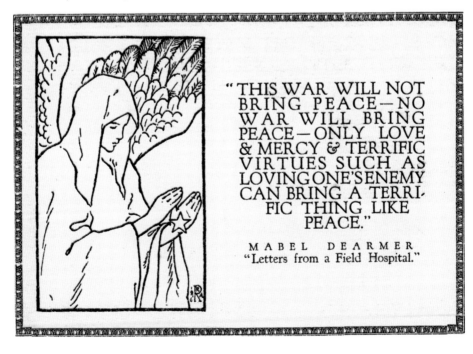

"THIS WAR WILL NOT BRING PEACE—NO WAR WILL BRING PEACE—ONLY LOVE & MERCY & TERRIFIC VIRTUES SUCH AS LOVING ONE'S ENEMY CAN BRING A TERRIFIC THING LIKE PEACE."

MABEL DEARMER
"Letters from a Field Hospital."

The First World War was opposed by many and initially by the National Executive of the Labour Party, although their disagreements were ignored and overturned by the parliamentary party. Individual politicians like George Lansbury, Keir Hardie and Fenner Brockway were opposed to the war. Indeed, Brockway was imprisoned for his refusal to fight, suffering the harshest of treatment. Another, who was later to be jailed, was Bertrand Russell, for attacking Britain's rejection in 1917 of the German Peace Offer. Indeed, a Christmas card critical of the war was produced by Russell.

Other Christmas Cards were also produced for the 'No Conscription Fellowship' formed in 1915. In 1916, voluntary enlistment ended and conscription with a 'conscience clause' allowing the right to claim exemption was introduced. The exemption clause was not an easy option as those who were imprisoned experienced horrendous conditions. Harold Bing recalls that some 'died in prison; some went mad; some broke down in health completely and never really recovered; some were discharged because they were on the point of death; some suffered terribly from insomnia ...'.[6] One of the cards by Percy Horton, a Conscientious Objector, shows someone in prison, embraced by an 'angel'.

Other Conscientious Objectors took up non-combative duties on the front line; as with prison, this was not an easy option and had very high casualty rates.

One of the most poignant symbols of the futility of the First World War was highlighted in a Christmas card of British and German soldiers leaving their trenches to share their cigarettes and play a game of football together in 'No-Man's Land', only to return to their

Above left: Artwork by British artist Soren Hawkes MA. Contact: passchendaelle@yahoo.co.uk.

Above right: 'Presented by the women of the Bombay Branch.' Printed and published by *The Times* Press, Bombay.

trenches and start the killing again. This theme was taken up in the film *War Horse* where the soldiers from opposing sides came together to rescue a horse who was also a victim of war. Unlike those who gave the orders to kill, it is likely that these soldiers had recognised their common bonds. Tragically, 10 million died and many more were injured before the carnage was over.

A line from Wilfred Owen's poem entitled 'Strange Meeting' seems apt for this occasion: 'I am the enemy you killed, my friend'.[7] Harry Patch, who was the longest surviving soldier to have fought in the trenches, further developed this sentiment, declaring that 'war is nothing but organised murder'.[8]

Yet the deaths, torture and horrendous physical and mental injuries are very rarely portrayed in official Christmas cards; instead, war is often presented in a humorous or patriotic way.

Meanwhile, in the Middle East, the British campaign in Iraq suffered a severe setback at the hands of the Turks. In 1917, Britain had more success and managed to capture Baghdad. After the war they imposed the Hashemite monarchy on Iraq. If the casual observer still believes that the West's interest in Iraqi oil is a relatively new phenomenon, then they are mistaken. As Nicholas Wood reminds us, 'in 1921 British Iraqi Petroleum Company, a consortium of the Shell Group, Anglo Persian, the French Government's Compagnie Francaise des Petroles, the American Near East Development Corporation and Mr Gulbenkian, [had a] total oil monopoly in Iraq ...'[9] What applied to Iraq pertains equally to Iran with ownership by the British Government of the majority of Iranian oil in the first half of the twentieth century.

Notes on Chapter 2

1. Keir Hardie, quoted in *J. Keir Hardie* by W. Stewart, Cassell & Son Ltd, 1921.
2. Emmaline Pankhurst quoted in *The Vote. How it was Won and How it was Undermined*, Viking, 2005.
3. Christabel Pankhurst quoted in *The Vote. How it was Won and How it was Undermined*, Viking 2005
4. Mrs Pankhurst, quoted in *The Vote, How it was Won and How it was Undermined*, Viking, 2005.
5. Adela Pankhurst quoted in *Peace Diary 1994*.
6. Harold Bing, quoted in 'Learn Peace' – a Peace Pledge Union Project.
7. 'Strange Meeting' by Wilfred Owen
8. Harry Patch
9. Nicholas Wood, *War Crimes or Just War 2003-2005*, South Hill Press, 2005.

CHAPTER 3

Conflict – Home and Abroad

To Fight
To Struggle
To Right the Wrong

– Alfred Lord Tennyson [1]

The years immediately following the First World War, like many before it, were dominated by a militancy which shocked many in power. The period, particularly from 1918 to 1921, became known as the 'Great Unrest'. It was a time of mass unemployment, with all the harshness and deprivation that went with it. It was also a period when many were expressing the values subscribed by the Labour Movement.

Still on the subject of values and collective action was a Christmas card produced by Young Socialists a few years earlier in 1918, highlighting children dancing and singing to the words 'Hand to hand, how far we reach, each for all and all for each. Thus we play and thus we teach – hearts and hands together.'

For just a few months in 1924, there was the first Labour Government headed by Ramsay McDonald, though without a parliamentary majority and dependent on Liberal support.

Another card, for which there is no date, but which presumably was created to reflect the conditions of this period, was accompanied by the words of Thomas Hardy, 'The pale pathetic people still plod on – through hoodwinking to light ...'

A Christmas card which was sent out by the National Union of Musical Instrument Makers in the early 1920s seems to reflect the struggles of the period, giving advice for the future with the words, 'it matters not how deep entrenched the wrong, how hard the battle goes, the day how long. Feint not, fight on! Tomorrow comes the song.'

Meanwhile, 'Not a penny off the pay, Not a second on the day,' was the cry of defiance which went out from the miners in response to the wish of Tory Prime Minister Stanley Baldwin and their employers to cut their wages and increase their hours, together with the withdrawal of subsidies by the government. A General Strike was called in May 1926 and within days, industry after industry ground to a halt, as workers came out in solidarity. The response from the government, as G. D. H. Cole describes, was 'armed special constables in thousands ... troops and reservists and ... what was practically an incitement to violence in the form of a promise of full support to these auxiliaries in acts they might commit in repressing the strike. It [the government] arrested and imprisoned hundreds of strikers under the Emergency Powers Act ...'[2]

Hand to hand, how far we reach, Each for all, and all for each;
Thus we play, and thus we teach — Hearts and hands together.

Christmas . and New Year 1918
Greetings and "Peace Wishes" from the YOUNG SOCIALIST.   L. L. & F. G. FOSTER

Above: P. J. Bourne.

Below left: Artist: JFH.

Below right: National Union of Musical Instrument Makers.

"The pale pathetic peoples still plod on
Through hoodwinkings to light……"
Thomas Hardy, "The Dynasts"

Greetings from Frank & Winifred Horrabin,
127 Hamlet Gardens,
Ravenscourt Park, W.

Be Strong!
It matters not how deep intrenched the wrong,
How hard the battle goes, the day how long.
Faint not, fight on! To-morrow comes the Song.

With the Season's
Greetings
and
Good Wishes
from
C. R. COLLIER.

376, GRAY'S INN ROAD,
LONDON, W.C.1.

May God, Good Will
and Good Neighbourhood
be your Company
Stanley Baldwin
Xmas 1928.

Left: Stanley Baldwin Xmas 1928.

Below: Old Comrades of the Miners' March – from the collection at Swansea University, donated by the late Nina Fishman.

The strike was solid and rapidly growing, but after just ten days, the leadership of the TUC called an end to it. They performed the role of servants to the Tory Government and the employers, while treating their own members with disdain. The miners continued to strike until November, eventually being starved back to work on conditions they had been fighting against.

Even allowing for this massive set back, G. D. H. Cole stated that '… it is arguable that it was preferable from the workers standpoint to strike and be defeated, than to give way without a struggle … given a clear enough indication of their will to resist … it can hardly be doubted … wages would have been reduced in the following years far more drastically than they were in fact reduced …'[3]

The workers' response to attacks on their living standards, with poverty and unemployment increasing, came in a number of different forms. Unemployment marches, petitions and other forms of direct action, increasingly began to capture the popular imagination. One such example, as a Christmas card highlights, was the Hunger March from South Wales to London.

A cartoon by Jax taken from the *New Leader*, 21 December 1934 and part of the WCML collection. The Working Class Movement Library, 51 Crescent Salford M5 4WX.

The Great Depression in the USA had an immediate effect on the UK, with the financial system facing collapse. One Christmas card appropriately published in 2010 takes a poster from the 1930s which highlighted the crisis of that period.

Other cards sent by Harriet Slater (who was later to become an MP), using verse from other writers, was meant at the time as a reminder of what the Labour Movement should be all about, together with the challenges and conditions faced. The words include 'you hold the whole world in your hand, see to it what you do'. The assumption has been made that these three cards were produced during this period but unfortunately we have been unable to verify the actual publication dates.

Questions relating to the British arms industry were also raised in a Labour Party poster of 1929, which, many years later, came to form the basis of a Christmas card. Neither the card nor the sentiments expressed could have been supported years later by New Labour. Indeed in their last year in office (2010) so-called defence expenditure reached £ 33 billion and like the present Coalition they were willing to export weapons of war to the most odious regimes.

Some years later, another Christmas card showed George Lansbury, who resigned the leadership of the Labour Party in 1935 over the issue of war and rearmament. Just a year earlier, he supported the birth of the Peace Pledge Union, which was committed to renouncing 'war and never again directly or indirectly will we support or sanction another.'[4]

As a pacifist, Lansbury had always shown himself to be a man of principle; an opponent of both the Boer and the First World War, a supporter of the suffragettes and a campaigner against poverty.

A Comrade's Greeting   For   A Happy Christmas

.........."The Challenges to be met and overcome are no smaller ; the demands upon those who would serve no lighter than they have ever been. Who would have it otherwise ? This is a companionship summoned for no mean or paltry purpose but for one of the great causes of history.

No service is too great for such a cause, for it is the cause of all mankind. No enemy in the end defeat it, for it has allies in the hearts of men and women everywhere."

—"50 Years March"

From :— *Harriet Slater*   "Hebor,"
Market Street, Milton,
Stoke-on-Trent

M P- Stoke on Trent

A Comrade's Greeting
for
A Happy Xmas and
A Prosperous New Year

Let me but live my life from year to year
With forward face and unreluctant soul !
Not hurrying to, nor turning from the goal ;
Not mourning for the things that disappear
In the dim past, nor holding back in fear
From what the future veils ; but with a whole
And happy heart that pays its toll
To Youth and Age, and travels on with cheer.

Henry Van Dyke

From :— *Harriet Slater*   "Hebor,"
Market Street, Milton,
Stoke-on-Trent.

A Comrade's Greeting
for
A Happy Xmas and
A Prosperous New Year

"Shall you complain who feed the world,
Who clothe the world, who house the world ?
Shall you complain who are the world,
Of what the world may do ?

The world's life hangs on your right hand,
Your strong right hand, your skilled right hand,
You hold the whole world in your hand,
See to it what you do."

From :— *Harriet Slater*   "Hebor,"
Market Street, Milton,
Stoke-on-Trent

A Comrade's Greeting – artist unknown – sent by Harriet Slater.

"WHEN THEY KEEP GIVING ME NEW TOYS ISN'T IT NATURAL THAT I'D WANT TO PLAY WITH 'EM?"

DON'T TOUCH

Presents from PEACE LOVING NATIONS

WAR

POISON GAS

1929 Labour Party poster

A peaceful Christmas to <u>all</u> the world's children

Above left: Ern Shaw 1929 Labour party poster. Published by the Labour Party, 150 Walworth Road, London SE17 1JT. Printed by Macdermot & Chant Ltd (TU) London and Welshpool.

Above right: From George Lansbury.

Right: 'Voluntarios Internacionales De Libertad.' Diana, Artes Gráficas (UGT), Larra, 6, Madrid; artist unknown.

A YEAR OF WORLD-WIDE VICTORY OVER FASCISM!

CHRISTMAS IN SPAIN

Bring to the dark Madonna no more myrrh,
Bring to her Child
No gold or frankincense.   To him and her
Lead no more asses piled
With jars of spikenard and bales of silk.
But to them bring
Lavishly gifts of milk.   Oh bring them milk
Swiftly, shepherd and king !
Lest the dark mother waking in the morn
of Christmastide
Sees on her bosom not the Christ new-born,
But Christ the crucified.

ELEANOR FARJEON

From Philip S. Bagwell.

Above: 'Christmas in Spain.' – Artist unknown.

Left: 'Voluntarios Internacionales De Libertad 1936-1937.' – Artist unknown.

Above left and right: W. J. Bassett-Lowke – courtesy of Northamptonshire Records Office, ZB498/21 and ZB498/22.

Right: Adolf Hitler. Artist – Laurie Tayler, Raphael Tuck & Sons, England, Series No. 8.

Meanwhile in Spain, the period had been dominated by the attempted military coup under the fascist leadership of General Francisco Franco, against the democratically elected Republican Government. The fascists received military assistance, with the provision of aircraft and such like from Germany and Italy. Sadly there was no such support from Britain for the Republican Government's defence of democracy from these forces of fascism. No such hesitation or renunciation of democracy was shown by the many anti-fascists from many parts of the world who went to Spain to fight alongside those in the Republican army. These included members of the International Brigade, who showed the kind of support that should have been forthcoming from their governments. The defeat of the Republican Government by the fascists opened the way for Hitler, the Nazis and the Second World War.

The Second World War was the bloodiest of wars. As with the First World War, there were those who, for a variety of reasons, refused to fight. The Peace Pledge Union estimates that there were 60,000 objectors, with approximately 3,000 being sent to prison. Some of the objectors were to work on farms, in hospitals and in other occupations, while others took up non-combative roles in the armed services, such as medics or bomb disposers. Many of these people, like the soldiers, were killed. It is important to emphasise that the pacifists did not support Nazism and the horrors which came with it; they simply opposed all wars, believing that the most important issue was the need to create a world in which all human life is valued. One card by an opponent of the war shows world leaders preaching peace, while practising war. This tradition of hypocrisy has carried on to the present day. Another card, produced in 1940, calls upon the 'warring countries to "light up" and St Christopher resume his good work for international fellowship.'

This card highlights opposition to Hitler through the use of ridicule, which can be the most difficult for a politician to counteract.

Notes on Chapter 3

1. Alfred Lord Tennyson, *'Wages' in Poems of Alfred Lord Tennyson, Vol. II*, edited by Hallam, Lord Tennyson. The Eversley Edition, 1908.
2. G. D. H. Cole, *A Short History of the British Working Class Movement 1789-1947*, George Allen and Unwin, London, 1960.
3. G. D. H. Cole, *A Short History of the British Working Class Movement 1789-1947*, George Allen and Unwin, London, 1960.
4. Peace Pledge Union Declaration, 1934.

CHAPTER 4

One War Ends, But Still No Peace On Earth

'I dream of giving birth to a child, who will ask, mother, what was war?'[1]

– Eve Merriam

With the end of the Second World War, it was assumed by many that after the victory over Nazi Germany, Winston Churchill would be swept back into office as the Prime Minister in the election of 1945. That was not to be; Clement Attlee, who had been Deputy Prime Minister in the war years, won with a massive parliamentary majority.

Following the end of the war, one of the issues that had to be dealt with was 'war crimes'. It was agreed to set up a tribunal at Nuremberg to deal with these crimes. They included 'Crimes against Peace, War Crimes and Crimes against Humanity and of a Common Plan or Conspiracy to commit those crimes.'[2]

One of the Nazi leaders to be tried was Hermann Goering, whose record is 'filled with admissions of his complicity in the use of slave labour'. He was accused of the destruction and plunder of occupied territory; shooting civilians and scattering populations; and of helping engineer the Final Solution against the Jews. He was 'found guilty on all accounts.'[3]

The Christmas card shows him languishing in prison, seemingly under the watchful eye of Hitler. However, Goering committed suicide before he could be hanged for his crimes.

With the end of the Second World War came the division of Germany into East and West. This Christmas card, produced a few years later, reflects the so-called Communist East being dreary and lacking in material goods, compared to a buoyant and prosperous West.

After the tens of millions of deaths, other casualties and refugees arising from the Second World War, one would have hoped that leaders the world over would then concentrate on planning for peace and not the next war. If they had done so, then the words later to be expressed by Bertrand Russell, could have begun to become a reality:

If the world could live for a few generations without war, war could come to seem as absurd as duelling has come to seem to us. No doubt there would be some homicidal maniac, but they would no longer be heads of government.[4]

The post-war message of peace, as so often happened in the past, was quickly forgotten or conveniently ignored when money and profits were at stake. As so many wars seem to be more concerned about financial rewards for the few, as opposed to issues of justice, we should not have been surprised by British troops being in Iraq in 1946. As with other wars

Above: Clem Atlee by Raphael Tuck & Sons Ltd, Christmas 1949.

Left: From the collection of The People's History Museum, Manchester.

Above: Divided Berlin. Artist: Jung.

Right: British troops in Iraq,
produced by GHQ Persia.

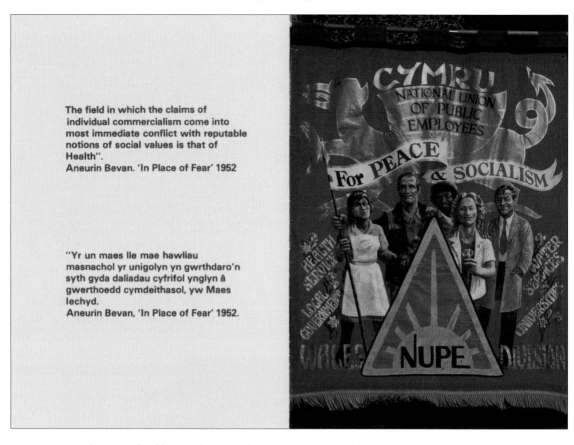

The field in which the claims of individual commercialism come into most immediate conflict with reputable notions of social values is that of Health".
Aneurin Bevan. 'In Place of Fear' 1952

"Yr un maes lle mae hawliau masnachol yr unigolyn yn gwrthdaro'n syth gyda daliadau cyfrifol ynglyn â gwerthoedd cymdeithasol, yw Maes Iechyd.
Aneurin Bevan, 'In Place of Fear' 1952.

National Union of Public Employees Wales (NUPE) Divisional Banner. Designed and produced by Mike Jones of Art Workers Cooperative.

with Iraq in both centuries, the reason remains the same – oil.

The latter part of the 1940s witnessed the birth of the National Health Service (NHS), with Aneurin Bevan as the Minister responsible. The justification for the creation of this service was summed up by Nye in one sentence, 'No society can legitimately call itself civilised if a sick person is denied medical aid because of lack of means.'[5] Although we were unable to find a card to commemorate the birth of the NHS, the Trade Union, NUPE, produced one many years later.

Returning to the subject of war, the three-year Korean War, starting in 1950, was seemingly being fought over the 38th Parallel, which divided North from South. If that was the reason, then it was a failure, as the demarcation line at the end of the war was identical to that at the beginning of the conflict. It was the first war fought in the name of the United Nations.

Yet, not only was the war not won by either side, it was lost in the most horrendous way with millions dying on both sides. *The Times*, reporting on the atrocities committed at the time, said, 'All the complaints against the People's Government of North Korea could be levelled against the South Korean Government ... The only difference is that at present, men and women accused of being communists, or of collaborating with the People's Government are being killed or imprisoned under the United Nations flag ...'[6] It could have been worse; General MacArthur wanted to invade China and use the Atomic bomb against the so-called enemy.

The Christmas cards below were sent by the North to the mainly American (and some British) soldiers who were fighting on behalf of the South. The purpose was to demoralise them and encourage them to go home to their families instead of fighting an unjust war where only the 'capitalists' would benefit.

Through their Christmas cards, the *Daily Worker*, the Communist Party newspaper, captured the austerity and continuing class divide in the UK. For example, they would use the words of Charles Dickens, to highlight that class relationship:

> I declare I never go into what is called 'Society' but I am not a-weary of it, despise it, hate it, and reject it. The more I see of its extraordinary conceit and its stupendous ignorance of what is passing out of doors, the more certain I am that it is approaching the period when, being incapable of reforming itself, it will have to submit to being reformed by others.

Another card, 'Among the Angels', quotes from *An Unfinished Story*, where humour is used to highlight the values of society:

Mr. Moneybags is in Florida this Christmas.

Where are you?   In Korea!
You risk your life, Big Business rakes in the dough.

Korea – from the Chinese People's Volunteers. No artist or publisher quoted.

CHRISTMAS –
HOME –
HAPPINESS –

Those who love you want you back home, safe and sound.

FIND A WAY OUT!

It's No Disgrace To Quit Fighting
In
This Unjust War!

傳单－118

Frozen rations eaten on the run.
Any moment he may have to run again,
to fight or die – and so may you.

Above and below: Korea – No artist or publisher quoted.

Dear Soldiers,
It is Christmas and you are far from home, suffering from cold not knowing when you will die.
The big shots are home enjoying themselves, eating good food, drinking good liquor, why should you be here risking your life for their profits?
The Koreans and Chinese don't want to be your enemies. Our enemies and yours are those who sent you here and destroyed your happiness.
Soldiers! Let's join hands!
You belong back home with those who love you and want you back, safe and sound. So we wish you ···········

"I declare I never go into what is called 'Society,' but I am not a-weary of it, despise it, hate it, and reject it. The more I see of its extraordinary conceit and its stupendous ignorance of what is passing out of doors, the more certain I am that it is approaching the period when, being incapable of reforming itself, it will have to submit to being reformed by others *Off the Face of the Earth*"

Charles Dickens

in a letter to his friend Foster

With Greetings

Charles Dickens
on the Ruling Class
A thought for Christmas

Prepared by the Bazaar Committee and sold on behalf of the *Daily Worker* Fighting Fund.

... as I said before, I dreamed that I was standing near a crowd of prosperous-looking angels, and a policeman took me by the wing and asked if I belonged to them; 'Who are they?' I asked.

'Why,' said he, 'they are the men who hired working girls, and paid 'em five or six dollars a week to live on. Are you one of that bunch?'

'Not on your immorality' said I, 'I'm only the fella that set fire to an orphan asylum and murdered a blind man for his pennies.'

Another Christmas card, 'Xmas Greetings', is obviously meant to portray a family from the prosperous end of the class divide with money in abundance to purchase the presents, which others who are less fortunate were denied.

This card is a role reversal, with the *Daily Worker* represented by happy twins at the top of the tree, while the big press barons are looking glum at the bottom.

This is followed by a reader (Ernest Bevin?) of the *Daily Worker*, wrapped in the American flag, ignoring the preying eyes of Churchill.

The other Christmas card shows a defiant worker, holding high the red flag, while taking scissors, presumably to Ernest Bevin, the Labour Government Minister, dressed as Santa Claus.

The *Daily Worker*, through their Christmas cards, was to continue to project the message of peace.

Sadly, but not surprisingly, this was not to be; plans were made by in the USA, Soviet Union and Britain for even more horrendous conflict by the development of even deadlier atomic, hydrogen and nuclear weapons.

Among the Angels

A thought for Christmas

Xmas Greetings !

Xmas Greetings

Above left: Prepared by the Bazaar Committee and sold on behalf of the *Daily Worker* Fighting Fund.

Left and above right: Issued by the Peoples Press Printing Society, publishers of the *Daily Worker.*

Top: *Daily Worker*. Artist: Patrick, 1949.

Middle: *Daily Worker.*

Bottom: With compliments, Young Communist League.

Photo by Glyn Ford.

The development of these weapons showed that not only had these leaders not learned the lessons from the war, but more specifically, from the catastrophic consequences of the atomic bombing of Hiroshima and Nagasaki. Over two hundred thousand were killed immediately, tens of thousands dying later as a direct result of radiation poisoning. Others experienced the most horrendous injuries.

These immoral acts of barbarism were not even necessary as General (later President) Eisenhower argued, 'Japan was at that moment seeking some way to surrender with minimum loss of face. It was not necessary to hit them with that awful thing.'[7] Many years later, a Christmas card was produced entitled 'Hand-folded paper cranes for peace'. The significance of this card is that a 'little Japanese girl, slowly dying of the effects of the 1945 bomb on Hiroshima, made herself hundreds of bright folded paper cranes. By tradition, they express the wish for life and good health – a sort of "get well card". Her efforts caught the imagination of the Hibakusha (bomb survivors) who adopted the symbol in 1957.'

If too many leading politicians were willing to fill the role of war mongers and worse still, nuclear war mongers, then others refused to follow that lead and developed campaigning groups to make their voices heard. This alternative message of peace was most appropriately reflected in the Christmas card and its traditional call for 'peace and goodwill'. As wars continued to rage, this message was as relevant as ever.

If 'peace and goodwill' are the words we normally associate with Christmas, then the usual image would be the dove. Its origins go back to biblical times, with the story of the flooding of the earth and the use of the dove to search for dry land, culminating in its return carrying an olive branch. This symbol to project the message of peace was used by Picasso and later by a leading Italian Communist artist, Renato Guttuso, in a Christmas card designed specifically for the *Daily Worker*. Significantly, the card is signed by the

PEACE ON EARTH

Above: Designed by Renato Guttuso for the *Daily Worker.*

Below left: Produced by The Peace Shop Ltd. Printed by Fingerprints (TU)56 Mackintosh Place, Cardiff.

Below right: Artist: Wendy Lewis.

leading British communist of that period, Harry Pollitt. It was sent to another prominent communist, Monty Johnson.

In the latter part of the 1950s, the Campaign for Nuclear Disarmament (CND) took the leading role in the anti-nuclear weapons movement.

CND's logo was to appear on Christmas cards often with the dove, reflecting the seasonal message of peace, while highlighting the insanity of the nuclear arms race and CND's determination to help bring it to an end. The logo was first used in 1958 on the 50-mile march between London and the Atomic Bomb factory at Aldermaston.

At the recent 50th Anniversary event at Aldermaston, the son and daughter of Gerald Holtom, the designer of this logo, reminded us that this peace symbol means 'get rid of your nuclear weapons'.[8] They also recalled their father 'emphasising the importance of the semaphore letter "U", seen in the upside down version of the peace symbol, representing unilateral action and the responsibility of the individual ... that when the world is nuclear free, the inverted symbol would also represent hands held up to rejoice ...'[9]

This card was not produced at the 'introduction' of the CND symbol but portrays it with a Christmas flavour.

There was an optimistic end to the decade of the 1950s with the overthrow in 1959 of Fulgencio Batista in Cuba, a friend of the United States Government and American mafia. He was replaced by leaders of the 'revolutionary left', headed by Fidel Castro, with his brother Raul and of course, Che Guevara.

This Christmas card, although not produced at the time of the revolution, highlights the continuing opposition to the Cuban regime from countries like the USA, even to the present day. Thankfully that opposition has not been successful and the revolution still survives, being an inspiration for several other Latin American countries.

Notes on Chapter 4

1. Eve Merriam, quoted in *Peace Diary 2009*, Housemans, London.
2. Quoted in Nicholas Wood, *War Games or Just War? The Iraq War 2003-2005*, South Hill Press, 2005.
3. Quoted in Nicholas Wood, *War Games or Just War? The Iraq War 2003-2005*, South Hill Press, 2005.
4. Bertrand Russell, *Has Man a Future?* Penguin, 1961.
5. Aneurin Bevan quoted in Michael Foot's biography on Bevan, Peladin Grenada, 1975.
6. James Cameron, *Point of Departure*, Penguin, 1961.
7. President Eisenhower, 16 April 1953, quoted in *Bombing Ahead With Disarmament*, Llew Smith MEP and Dr David Lowry, 1989.
8. CND Website http://www.cnduk.org/
9. Dawn Rothwell interviewing Darius and Rebecca Holtman, CND Newsletter.

CHAPTER 5

Days of Hope

My brain socialist.
My heart anarchist.
My eyes pacifist.
My blood revolutionary.[1]

– Adrian Mitchell

The 1960s, at least in the western industrialised world, was a decade of hope and increasing confidence in our ability not only to challenge the establishment, but to replace it with a far more just and peaceful world. That required people to make history with their own set of values, and not stand idly by as others imposed their beliefs on them.

Many individuals and groups throughout much of the world made up this movement, or movements for change, with the hippies, the flower power people, the anti-Vietnam War activists, peace mongers, nuclear disarmers, civil rights campaigners, anti-racists, anti-apartheid activists, socialists, students, trade unionists, together with many poets and musicians, whose songs were sung as they marched 'onwards to victory'.

CND continued throughout the sixties and, particularly in the first few years of that decade, increased in both size and intensity. The Aldermaston March was the main focus of the activities. Over 100,000 marched. The question was sung, 'Can You Hear the H-bomb thunder?' and the answer was given, 'Yes'. They committed themselves to the belief that 'We Shall Overcome'.

Yet others within CND, particularly Bertrand Russell, were of the opinion that what was needed was more direct action to confront the nuclear menace. He and others were to form the 'Direct Action Committee', which attempted to bring a stop to work at nuclear bases. This body was then superceded by the 'Committee of 100', committed to civil disobedience and, where necessary, law breaking against the nuclear arms race. Russell was jailed along with others for his activities. His views on the role of law breaking were expressed as far back as 1936, stating:

> All great advances have involved illegality. The early Christians broke the law; Galileo broke the law; the French revolutionaries broke the law and early trade unionists broke the law. The instances are so numerous and so important that no-one can maintain as an absolute principle, obedience to a constituted authority.[2]

Russell continued to warn of the dangers of nuclear war, as he had in the past, saying:

Design by Robin Martin.

It may well be that the next war will end with the stronger side still possessing H-Bombs, but neither side possessing live human beings …[3]

In the UK, after thirteen years of Tory government, the electorate decided that 'enough was enough' and in 1964 a Labour government was elected, with Harold Wilson as Prime Minister. Yet the majority was still only in single figures and in 1966 they were forced to call another General Election, returning with a substantial majority.

Another war that began to command public attention was the USA's invasion of Vietnam. Opposition to the war took many forms and covered much of the world, including the United States, where the government was faced by both desertions and refusals to serve, often highlighted with the burning of draft cards. Opposition also took the form of massive demonstrations worldwide. One of the largest of these was in London, which culminated in near riots at Grosvenor Square, 'Hey, Hey, LBJ, How Many Kids Have you Killed Today?' was a popular chant during such marches. There was a total silence from the USA administration wherever and whenever this question was raised. If there was still any doubt as to whose side the demonstrators were on, they also chanted, 'Ho, Ho, Ho, Chi Minh'.

The first of these Christmas cards is a typical USA regimental one aimed at the North Vietnamese with the words, 'Let Freedom Ring'. Ironically, the card also included the words 'peace on earth, goodwill to all men' although, at the time, the USA was bombing the Vietnamese with napalm.

The other card with the opposite viewpoint comes from the Provisional Revolutionary Republic, demanding that the 'Nixon administration ends its war of aggression in Vietnam.'

Yet another card ridicules the decision to award Kissinger the Nobel Prize for Peace, even though he was a rabid advocate of US aggression, including against Vietnam. The card poses the question 'Where will the Dove of Peace strike next?'

Above left: United States Military Assistance Command.

Above right: Provisional Revolutionary Government of South Vietnam.

Right: Alan Hardman.

Above: Freedom Charter by Paul Morton. Leeds Postcards, PO Box 84 Leeds LS1 4HU.

Left: Produced by NICRA Northern Ireland Civil Rights Association 1975.

Produced by The Grand Orange Lodge of Ireland.

Birmingham Six: 'Remember them this Christmas.'

Furthermore, a high profile campaign was to emerge and grow in the late 1960s, continuing for many years against the system of apartheid in South Africa; a system based on white minority rule, beginning officially in 1948, but in reality, going back much further to the Dutch and British colonial times.

Much to the surprise of many people, Edward Heath's Tories defeated Labour in the 1970 General Election.

In the early 1970s, a renewal of the conflict in Northern Ireland emerged with demonstrations often highlighting the continued discrimination against Catholics. Sadly, the conflict in Northern Ireland escalated with killings on both sides.

A Christmas card was produced by the Northern Ireland Civil Rights Association, humorously showing the arrest system, but with Santa as the victim. This body had been formed in 1967, and its list of demands included: one-man one-vote in local elections; the removal of gerrymandered boundaries; laws against discrimination by local government; allocation of public housing on a points system; repeal of the Special Powers Act and disbanding of the part-time 'B' Specials.

It is interesting to note that, unlike the Republicans, the Unionists rarely produced Christmas cards with an overtly political message.

Meanwhile, the conflict in Northern Ireland came to mainland Britain with bombs being planted in two pubs in Birmingham in 1974, causing twenty-one deaths and 182 injuries. A number of men were found guilty of these deaths. A campaign was mounted to demonstrate their innocence and a Christmas card was printed as a reminder of their continued plight. Eventually, the campaign succeeded and they were released, but not before they had spent sixteen years in prison.

Photograph courtesy of *The Morning Star.*

Meanwhile on the industrial front, the government suffered a massive defeat by the NUM over their pay demand; they were also forced to release the five dockers who had been imprisoned under the Industrial Relations Act for contempt of court.

This was followed by a national building strike, which resulted in the award of the biggest ever pay increase, although they failed to end the 'lump', where workers get paid cash-in-hand, a system which prevented effective trade unionism. Following the strike, the Home Secretary, Robert Carr, asked chief constables to investigate trade union violence on the picket lines, following approaches from the National Federation of Building Trades Employers. Court cases followed, but not for any acts of violence; they found other reasons to charge them, such as conspiracy under the 1845 Act. Three of the members – Des Warren, Ricky Tomlinson and McKinsie Jones – were found guilty and sentenced to imprisonment. Others were found guilty and imprisoned for other offences. Although receiving little support from their union leadership, many of the grass roots members protested with demonstrations and strikes.

The campaign against these miscarriages of justice continues to this day, as it is increasingly recognised that they were victims of trumped up charges and now deserve to have their names cleared.

Industrial action continued and culminated in the events of 1974, with the miners just a few days away from striking. Edward Heath and the Tories decided to take them on by calling a General Election on the question of 'who runs the country?' Going by the result, whoever it was, it was not Heath; the Tories were defeated and a Labour government was elected. Wilson was once again to be the Prime Minister and the dispute was settled.

Much to everyone's surprise, Harold Wilson was to resign as Prime Minister in 1976; Jim Callaghan won the subsequent leadership election.

Notes on Chapter 5

1. Adrian Mitchell, *For Beauty Douglas*, Allison and Busby, 1982.
2. Bertrand Russell, *Which Way to Peace*, Michael Joseph, 1936.
3. Bertrand Russell, *Russell's Best*, Unwin Paperbacks, 1981.

CHAPTER 6

Little Hope, No Jobs

'I will continue to be the essence of sweet reasonableness.'[1]

– Margaret Thatcher

Before entering 10 Downing Street for the first time as Prime Minister, Thatcher had the audacity to paraphrase St Francis of Assisi:

Where there is discord may we bring harmony.
Where there is error, may we bring truth.
Where there is doubt, may we bring faith and
Where there is despair, may we bring hope.[2]

Instead, the reality was a decade of despair and discord with no 'faith, hope or harmony'.

The quote paraphrasing St Francis of Assisi was in some respects similar to the sentiments expressed in the Tory election manifesto of 1979, promising that, 'The Conservative government's first job will be to rebuild our economy' and to 're-unite a divided and disillusioned people.'[3]

In contrast to 'rebuilding our economy', Thatcher and her government was responsible during her first term of office for :

- The worst level of unemployment ever seen in this country
- The worst slump in industry in 60 years
- A record number of companies going bust
- The lowest level of peacetime house building since the 1920s
- The highest tax burden ever imposed (for all but the rich)
- The fastest drop in living standards since the war
- The greatest raid ever on our future: investment in people and plant [4]

Although appalled by Thatcher's election, socialists were still pleased at the election of Michael Foot as Leader of the Labour Party, following the resignation of Jim Callaghan. The designer of this card also welcomed the election of Michael, portraying it as a present, a foot, in his Christmas stocking.

Labour then began to move more to the left and this found favour with the membership and the trade unions, but unfortunately not with a right-wing rump within the

Above left: Printed at the Labour Hall, New Bradwell, and published by Bradwell Branch of the Labour Party.

Above right: Artist: Steve Smith.

Parliamentary Labour Party. They struck back almost immediately with some prominent MPs resigning to form the Social Democratic Party (SDP).

While attempting to rebuild unity within the party in order to fight the next General Election, in reality, Michael's main task was to keep it together as a serious electoral force. This was achieved, but at the expense of getting his socialist economic message over to the electorate. Unlike some, he still remained true to his beliefs, especially his opposition to nuclear weapons, describing himself as an 'inveterate peace monger'.

The card with a clenched fist was also a reminder of the importance of sticking to socialist principles.

Meanwhile in 1981, Thatcher's Christmas card list included Saddam Hussein, the Iraqi dictator. She also described Muammar Gaddafi, the Libyan dictator, as 'The Leader of the Great First September Revolution'.

With the election of Thatcher, many became increasingly concerned that while they spoke of individual freedom, rights of association, speech and assembly, the Tories were in fact undermining them.

In Thatcher's proposed new world of peace and 'harmony', jobs in abundance were promised and not just any old jobs, but 'real jobs'.[5] She argued that Conservatives hate unemployment. Just a year later, while extolling the virtues of her new government to the Tory faithful, she informed her unquestioning audience that Conservative policies are the only ones which gave any hope of bringing the people back to real and lasting

Left: Artist: John Minnion, 1980. Published by Leeds Postcards, 13 Claremont Grove, Leeds. Printed by Tyneside Free Press.

Below: Artist: Maggie Guillon, devised by Trudy Begg.

employment. So strong were her beliefs in her programme, that by 1981 she was able to declare – incredibly – that, 'There are now clear signs that the worst of the recession is over.'[6] Meanwhile, back in the real world, unemployment was rocketing and by 1983 it had reached 3.2 million.

Unfortunately for Thatcher, as unemployment increased dramatically, fewer people were convinced by her message. Mass unemployment was having a dramatic and adverse effect on both the unemployed and employed. The unemployed experienced cuts in their standard of living, with the demoralisation that goes with the loss of a job. While for those who were in employment, the fear was that they too would experience a similar fate – the dole queue. The poverty which came with this was linked with that of Victorian times and the values Mrs Thatcher had previously admired.

So Thatcher's dream of 'real jobs' and 'harmony', had quietly been confined to the dustbin of history, being replaced by mass unemployment and the anti-trade union laws she had introduced in the early 1980s.

As for the trade unions, these developments obviously had a dramatic effect, weakening their bargaining position with management and deterring workers from taking industrial action.

Yet in 1982, the miners took industrial action in support of their wage claim. The government were not prepared and quickly conceded to the miners' demands.

Having shown her disinterest in the plight of the unemployed and her hatred of the trade unions, Thatcher then embarked on her journey to destroy the public sector. The latter was part of the Tories' programme, as Thatcher declared, to 'roll back the frontiers of socialism.'[7] In the years to come and with considerable justification, she was to claim that they had 'done more' to achieve this aim, 'than any previous Conservative Government.'[8]

Public housing was an area where she put this philosophy into practice and future generations increasingly became the victims of it. She ensured that the council house building programme was slashed, falling to its lowest level in any peace-time year since the 1920s; renovation for council houses was also dramatically cut; council house rents rocketed, while hundreds of thousands of workers were languishing on the dole. Perhaps the most damaging of all was the decision to sell off council houses, which had been built to respond to need. As a result of this action, social housing would be less available to people in need. Homeless families today are still living with the catastrophic consequences of her actions.

Next came the National Health Service, which was subject to cuts and privatisation by the Tories. In 1982, Sir Geoffrey Howe said of private health, 'we must encourage it to grow faster',[9] and in fact, it doubled from 1979 to 1983 and continues to the present day.

Yet in 1980, the Black Report had been published, linking many aspects of ill-health with poverty. Reluctant to admit to such a link, their response to the recommendations in the report for additional expenditure in the NHS was that it was 'quite unrealistic in the present or in any foreseeable circumstances'.[10]

Nor was it just in the health services and housing where resources were increasingly failing to keep up with demand, but also in education with 6 per cent cuts. Thatcher was seen to be reverting to type, 'snatching' from the poor, as she did when she was Secretary

Left and below: Artist: Maggie Guillon, devised by Trudy Begg.

Above: Artist: Maggie Guillon, devised by Trudy Begg.

Right: Artist: Steve Bell. Published by St Peter's Branch Labour Party. Printed by GMS Typing & Photocopying Service, 20 Argyle Road, Brighton.

Above left: Design: Alan Hardman. Printed by Revolution Graphics, 81 Troughton Rd, London SE7.

Above right: Recycled Images.

of State for Education in a previous Tory government, ending all free school milk. She was then known as 'Thatcher, the Milk Snatcher'. On a similar theme, Thatcher is portrayed reclaiming children's Christmas stockings.

Another card highlights the link between poverty and arms spending with Reagan expressing the opinion that 'Hunger's temporary, my child, but Freedom is forever'.

Still on the subject of the poorer sections of society, the attacks continued through Thatcher's taxation policies. Overall, taxes for the poor increased, being lowered for the rich.

Thatcher and her government also continued in other areas to attack the public sector, by the privatisation of a number of large public companies.

Privatisation was also being brought in the 'back door' in areas like health and education.

I have already referred to the West's involvement with Iran throughout the twentieth century and a part of that history was the storming of the American Embassy in Tehran with fifty-two staff members being held hostage for 444 days by Iranian revolutionary students, demanding the return of the Shah to face trial in Iran. The following year in London, embassy buildings were stormed, with hostages taken for different reasons and by opposing groups, demanding the release of ninety-one fellow Arabs from Ayatollah Khomeini's jails. People were invited to include a message to the hostages in Tehran in a Christmas card produced in the United States.

Thatcher and the Tories increased real military expenditure by 23.3 per cent in their first five years as well as agreeing to an expansion of our military nuclear capability by

HOWE INTOLERABLE

Ho! Ho! Ho! Sir Geoffrey has a special festive message for the nation this yuletide. Dismissing any suggestion of a "U-turn", Sir Geoffrey, who has fought a lonely, life-long, personal battle with stupidity, explained that the Chancellor's custom of giving presents to children at Xmas was "no longer viable". Instead Sir Geoffrey plans to give away the National Health Service and the education system to poor businessmen.

Sir Geoffrey Howe as Santa Claws

SAS 27. South Atlantic Souvenirs.

© Copyright 1979 Binghamton Press Company, Inc.

A Christmas Greeting From Home
Our Thoughts Are With You

To the American Hostages Held in the Embassy in Iran:

Merry Christmas!
SIGNED:

An American Citizen

A Public Service of The Binghamton, N.Y., Evening Press

Binghamton, NY, *Evening News*.

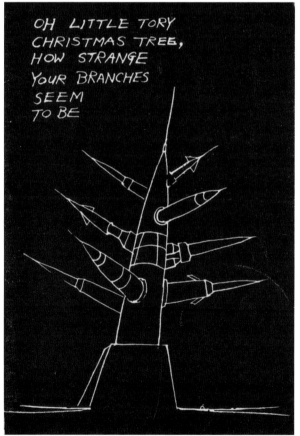

Above: A *Morning Star* card. Printed by Farleigh Press Ltd, Watford, Herts.

Left: Design: Alan Hardman. Printed by Revolution Graphics, 81 Troughton Rd, London SE7.

replacing Polaris with Trident. The danger of these weapons of mass destruction was imaginatively portrayed in the following cards.

They also took the decision to agree to American demands to place cruise missiles on British soil at Molesworth in Cambridgeshire and Greenham Common. In 1981, in response to this decision, a group of women, men and children walked the 125 miles from Cardiff to Greenham and proceeded to set up an all-women peace camp at the base. As Sarah Van Veen of the Greenham Peace Women was to say, 'In the past, men have left home to go to war. Now women are leaving home for peace.'[11]

They began to hit the headlines, particularly following the decision of the Courts in 1982 to find twenty-three of them guilty for occupying the security box under the main gate of the base, together with the obstruction of work on developing the base.

Demonstrations and forms of direct action continued, with many women living outside the base until after cruise missiles were removed.

These Christmas cards from Greenham in 1982 highlight one of the demonstrations, with the banner carrying a message to another woman, Margaret Thatcher: 'Here's your Christmas cheque. Don't spend it on bombs for the children.' Another card shows the banner: 'We have a Dream' – not just for the closure of Greenham, but also for a nuclear-free world.

Other cards were produced with one highlighting the devastation which would follow if cruise missiles were ever used.

Photograph: Brenda Prince.

Above: Designed and made by M. Heard for the Bath Star March to Greenham Common 13 July-6 August 1983. Photographer: I. Campbell.

Left: Artist: Paul Morton. On the First Day of 'Cruisemass'.

Artist: Paul Morton.

The following card highlights the closeness of Thatcher and Reagan as they progress on their military adventure on a sleigh ride over Europe.

Another, ignoring the Christmas spirit, has Thatcher responding to a plea for 'A Job for Daddy' with 'You'll get a Missile like everyone else.'

On the linked issue of nuclear power, these Christmas cards from the early 1980s show opposition to its development, particularly in response to the construction of a second nuclear plant at Sizewell in Suffolk.

Producers of some Christmas cards were quick to remind Thatcher of how the Tories apparently saw the traditional role of women as household prisoners.

In Thatcher's first term of office, Christmas cards were being sent representing the opposition to the military coup in Chile, headed by General Pinochet, which resulted in the overthrow of the democratically elected government and the murder of its President, Salvador Allende. The coup, supported by the USA Government and its CIA, continued to repress and murder the people in that country, and in particular, those such as trade unionists who continued to oppose the junta.

It is likely that none of those who sent these Christmas cards, asking for solidarity with the Chilean struggle, were under any illusions as to Thatcher's feelings. Indeed, many years later, when Pinochet was under house-arrest in Britain, she visited and thanked him for 'bringing democracy to Chile'.[12] This confirmed what Thatcher meant by democracy.

Meanwhile, in other parts of Latin America, the Tory Government merely acted as a poodle to the USA. They supported USA aggression against Nicaragua, while being equally

Above left: Artist: Alan Hardman. Revolution Graphics c/o 1 Mentmore Terrace, London E8 3PN.

Above right: Artist: Paul Morton.

Left: East Anglian Alliance Against Nuclear Power. 12 Groveside, Yoxford, Suffolk. Designed by Deborah Ardizzone.

Right: 'Merry Bloody Christmas' by Janet de Wagt. Leeds Postcards PO Box 84, Leeds, England LS1 4HU.

Below: Published by Chile Solidarity Campaign (1980), 127 Seven Sisters Road, London N7 7QG.

supportive of their close links to Guatemala and El Salvador's repressive regimes, as this card demonstrates.

The struggle against the apartheid regime continued in the early 1980s, although without the support of Thatcher and the Tories. Indeed, Thatcher expressed the wish to 'make progress towards ending the isolation of South Africa in world affairs.'[12] Her words were backed by action: the ban on North Sea oil exports to that country was lifted; firms paying starvation wages would not be made public; the apartheid regime was defended

Left: Design: Mediumwave for the Nicaraguan Solidarity Campaign.

Below: Artist: Steve Smith.

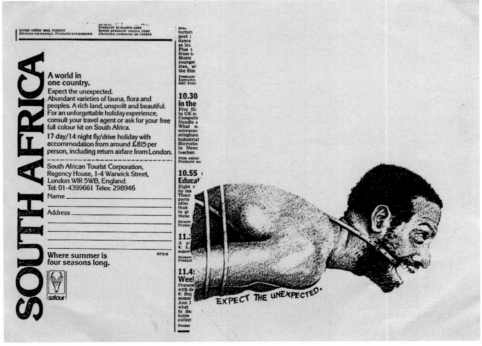

from censure in the Security Council of the United Nations, while ensuring the IMF loan to that country, was approved.

Thatcher, faced with near record levels of unemployment and with the economy in tatters, was rapidly becoming the most unpopular Prime Minister ever. Yet luck, or more accurately events at home and abroad, were to rescue her.

At home, as mentioned earlier, senior figures in the Parliamentary Labour Party left to set up the Social Democratic Party (SDP). The Labour Party was in turmoil and Michael Foot had the massive task of not just winning the next election, but also of maintaining the party as a viable force in British politics. Both the SDP and the Tories were the beneficiaries

Right: Artist: Alan Hardman.

Below: SAS 21. South Atlantic Souvenirs. Seasonal Art Series.

Bottom: 'Tory Cuts' cartoon by Maggie Guillon & Trudy Begg.

of this split. Michael still kept to Labour's anti-nuclear policy. He also began to tackle what he saw as the problem of the Militant Tendency.

Abroad, Thatcher received another massive electoral boost with the Falklands War. A war over sovereignty of an island 8,000 miles away from our shores and 400 miles from Argentina; the word 'imperialism' comes to mind!

The media in Britain supported and encouraged the war in the most jingoistic manner and succeeded in whipping up pro-war sentiment. Even the 'inveterate peace-monger' Michael Foot backed the war. Protests still occurred, but they were drowned out by the campaign for war. The fact that the arms suppliers, supported by the government, had supplied Argentina with some of their weapons of war was not regarded as particularly significant by the war mongers.

The final card of Thatcher's first term in office highlights what they see as 'achievements' and what others saw as 'disasters'.

Notes on Chapter 6

1. Margaret Thatcher quoted in 'Sound Bites' compiled by the New Internationalist
2. Margaret Thatcher, paraphrasing St Francis of Assisi, as she entered No. 10 Downing Street for the first time as Prime Minister in 1979.
3. Conservative Party Election Manifesto, 1979.
4. *Thatcher's Britain – A Guide to the Ruins*, published by Pluto Press and New Socialist.
5. Margaret Thatcher, 25 June 1981, quoted in *Thatcher's Britain*, various authors, Pluto Press, London, 1983.
6. Margaret Thatcher, 25 June 1981, quoted in *Thatcher's Britain*, various authors, Pluto Press, London, 1983.
7. Margaret Thatcher, quoted in *Thatcher's Britain*, various authors, Pluto Press, London, 1983.
8. Margaret Thatcher, 8 October 1982, quoted in *Thatcher's Britain*, various authors, Pluto Press, London, 1983.
9. Geoffrey Howe, 3 July 1982, quoted in *Thatcher's Britain*, various authors, Pluto Press, London, 1983.
10. Patrick Jenkins, 1980, quoted in *Thatcher's Britain*, various authors, Pluto Press, 1983.
11. Sarah Van Veen quoted in *Is the Future Tender? Troubled Thoughts on Contemporary Feminism*, Virago, London, 1987.
12. Margaret Thatcher, BBC, 26 March 1999.
13. Margaret Thatcher quoted in *Thatcher's Britain*, various authors, Pluto Press, 1983.

CHAPTER 7

Enemies Everywhere

'She has no imagination and that means no compassion.'[1]

– Michael Foot

With Thatcher's re-election in 1983 came the resignation of Michael Foot as Labour's leader. Michael had managed to keep the party together as a serious electoral force, but the defections of MPs to the SDP had caused enormous damage. This problem was made worse by some who remained in the party, including Jim Callaghan, who had recognised when he was Prime Minister that Michael had 'put aside his personal feelings in order to help our Party ...'[2] Callaghan had no intention of repaying the favour and in the middle of Michael's election campaign he spoke out against Labour's defence policy, which was already a most controversial issue in the election. It was a terrible act of treachery, helping to guarantee a Labour defeat.

Neil Kinnock succeeded Michael as leader; although much younger, he was still seen by many as also being on the 'left' of the party. However, he abandoned the commitment to withdraw from the Common Market and accepted that 'the market is potentially a powerful force for good'.[3] Following his and the Labour Party's defeat in the 1987 General Election, Neil then abandoned his commitment to unilateral nuclear disarmament.

One of the issues that Neil was to deal with, which had also concentrated Michael's mind, was the Militant Tendency, as indicated earlier, and its eventual expulsion from the party.

Meanwhile, with her re-election, an even more confident Thatcher was ready to take on her enemies, ranging from the public sector, the trade unions, the Soviet Union, Common Market, together with Mandela and the African National Congress. One could also add the majority of her own Cabinet to the list.

First, the public sector, with many industries and services being subject to various forms of privatisation, as the card portrays in a humorous way.

Also more cuts were made in other public services, including housing and health.

With St Francis of Assisi a thing of the past, the notion of 'harmony' was thrown out of the window and replaced by what seemed to be class war in her confrontation with the trade unions.

The first to be subject to her vitriol and attacks were the trade unions at the government's Communication Headquarters (GCHQ) in 1984, the government's spy listening centre, which worked in conjunction with MI5 and MI6. She obviously saw them as a threat to the State; but then, didn't she think that of all trade unionists?

SAS/Reindeer Times – Red Flag Over The Mersey 'series'. RMS 3.

"Apparently he's been privatised by a consortium of local businessmen."

Artist: Banx. Published by the Labour Party 150 Walworth Road London SE17 1JT and printed by Bell Press (TU) 5 Jeans Lane, Bells Hill, Bishop's Stortford, Herts, CM23 2NN.

Artist: Banx. Published by the Labour Party and printed by Bell Press.

Artist: Maggie Guillon, devised by Trudy Begg.

To break the union, bullying and bribery followed, with most members being transferred to other parts of the service or leaving it. Fourteen brave trade unionists stood their ground, refusing to resign their membership and the government responded by sacking them. But undeterred, they continued their campaign to highlight their plight and the government's refusal to recognise what should be a fundamental human right to be a member of a trade union. In 1997, with the election of the New Labour Government, the ban was lifted and some of the fourteen sacked workers returned to work. Others had already reached retirement age.

Nowhere was Thatcher's hatred of the unions and her determination to destroy them more obvious than in the 1984 Miners' Strike. Indeed, she compared the fight against the miners with the fight against the Argentinean junta, which had recently been defeated in the Falklands War. She set out, not just to defeat the miners, but to crush them, taking away their jobs and destroying their communities.

Thatcher was also determined that old scores – such as past union victories – should

Artist: Dee. Published by GCHQ Trade Unions and printed by Shadowdean Ltd (TU).

be settled. Unlike in the early 1980s, this time the government was prepared. The whole apparatus of the State was marshalled against the NUM, including a compliant, well-paid police force, which was more than willing to carry out the wishes of the government. This was then compounded by the use of non-union drivers to transport 'scabs' to the collieries and coal to power stations. Coal stocks had also been built up prior to the strike.

These and other factors resulted in a defeat for the miners after their year-long strike. If victory had been dependent on courage, on the commitment of the miners and their families, then the battle would have been won. Sadly, this was not so. With the defeat came the destruction of the industry – as the union had warned – together with the near destruction of many of the communities dependent on them.

One of these cards rightly highlights the crucial role played by the women's support group; other cards show those who opposed the strike, including the Tory Government, Ian MacGregor, Head of NCB, and most of the media.

Another tragic consequence of the defeat of miners, who had been sacked at the time of the strike, was the loss of not just their jobs but also the limited financial benefits of redundancy pay etc.

Even more tragic was a Christmas card produced many years later, recognising those who had 'lost their lives' supporting the struggle of the miners.

Yet the damage was to extend even further and in a different form, with the demoralisation of the miners increasingly extended to the wider trade union and labour movement. This, together with the mass unemployment of that time, led to a weakened trade union movement which, to this day, has still not recovered.

It is interesting, although sad, to note the similarities in Tory Government responses to the General Strike of 1926 and the Miners' Strike of 1984. Between the threat of a General Strike in 1925 and the Strike itself in 1926, the TUC had spent its time discussing and putting forward 'proposals to the Samuel Commission'[4] in the hope that the dispute could

Above left: Published by Notts Central Strike Fund. Printed by Ramoth.

Above right: Artwork by Steve Bell, published by Richmond and Twickenham Miners and Family Support Campaign.

Below: Christmas Appeal for Shirebrook Striking Miners, 1984.

Top: From Sherwood Colliery Women's Support Group.

Above: South Wales NUM, 1984.

Right: Artist: Alan Hardman.

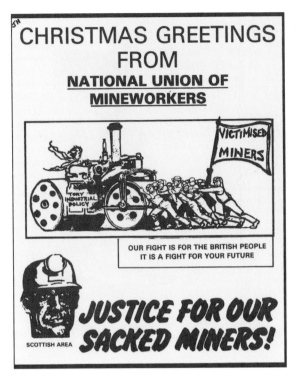

Above left: Published by the Scottish Miners Relief Fund.

Above right: From the NUM.

be resolved. The government, however, was in belligerent mood and the Commission gave them breathing space to prepare for the General Strike. When asked why they seemed to concede to the miners in 1925, the government's response was, 'We were not ready'.[5]

Similar reasoning also applied to the Thatcher Government in the 1980s. While not ready to take the miners on in 1982, the same did not apply in 1984. Like the Tory Government of 1925, they immediately used the period to prepare for the 1984 Miners' Strike. One of the other similarities between the General Strike of 1926 and the Miners' Strike of 1984 was the lack of support from the TUC.

On a more positive note, Tower Colliery in South Wales, which was to have been another victim of Thatcher's destruction of the mining industry, resisted the closure; the mine was kept open and running as a workers' co-operative. It continued as one until 2005, when it was no longer economic to mine coal. This later card was one of the many that I received during this period.

Another major strike was the one at Silent Night. Peter Pike MP in a parliamentary debate outlined the case for the workers. A Union which agreed to 'forego the pay rise' in return for a 'no redundancy agreement to run for a year' was then faced with 'the management' who 'broke the agreement and declared 52 redundancies.'[6]

Further defeats for the Labour Movement were to follow and few were more contentious than the dispute in the print industry, when Thatcher's friend, the equally ruthless Rupert Murdoch, moved all of his national newspapers from Fleet Street, where the unions were

Above left: From the Workforce and Directors of Tower Colliery.

Above right: Artwork: Red Ink. Produced by Burnley Labour Womens' Council for the families of Silentnight Strikers, 1986.

well organised, to Wapping. The strike and mass picketing which followed was, once again, met by a savage response from a compliant police force. This, and the use of non-union and 'scab' labour, ensured the continued production and distribution of the papers and the defeat of the union.

At Senior Colman Engineering there was another long strike. Ken Eastham MP, speaking in a parliamentary debate, explained that, 'The dispute arose because the management victimised four workers ...'[7]

On the international front, a Christmas card from 1984 is entitled: 'Chile: One More Push for Freedom'. It is made up of a 'passionate art of resistance' by 'women in the shanty towns of Santiago'. It portrays a 'day of protest', where 'shanty dwellers erect barricades of wood and burning tyres in protest against the dictatorship and for a return to democracy.' Thatcher would have showed no sympathy for the protest.

Other Christmas cards urge support for the liberation struggle in other Latin American countries, including Nicaragua.

Meanwhile, the nuclear menace still loomed, but surprisingly, in January 1986, Gorbachev announced proposals for the complete elimination of all nuclear weapons within fifteen years. Perhaps even more surprisingly, at a summit in Reykjavik in the October of that year, President Reagan seemed to be seriously considering moves in that direction. Together with Gorbachev, they seemingly came close, if not to a complete elimination, to very deep reductions in nuclear weapons. Sadly, for a number of reasons,

Right: Haringey Print Workers Support Group.

Below: South Atlantic Souvenirs.

Left: From the Senior Colman Strikers of Manchester.

Below: Published by Chile Solidarity Campaign (1984), 129 Seven Sisters Road, London N7 7QG.

Nicaragua Health Fund, 83 Margaret Street, London W1N 7HB.

Artist: Steve Smith.

Above left: Glyn Ford.

Above right: Artwork: Steve Bell.

including Thatcher's opposition, they failed, although it did lead to advances with agreement on International Nuclear Forces in 1987, which paved the way to achieving the Strategic Arms Reduction Treaty in 1991.

Meanwhile, Thatcher's priority was to build up our weapons of war.

Yet another card humorously portrays Thatcher and Reagan joining forces to declare war on Christmas.

One card shows what seems to be an out of character Father Christmas delivering missiles down the chimney. This seems similar to many governments, including those in the UK, who sell weapons of war to the most repressive regimes, who in turn use them against populations, including children.

By the following year, a wiser Santa Claus had joined CND and not only was he no longer delivering weapons of war to our children, but he was confiscating those he had delivered in previous years.

The Snowman's political development was even more rapid, extending 'Socialist Greetings' at Christmas. By the end of this book, most readers will be pleased to see that Santa had also joined the campaign for peace and socialism.

Rotting food caused by excessive wastage in a hungry world became increasingly difficult for those in authority to defend. The extent of the food surpluses in the EEC was highlighted in the figures on the card.

Above left: George Blair.

Above right: Artist unknown.

Below left: Artist: Alan Hardman.

Below right: Artist unknown.

Angela Martin, Leeds
Postcards, PO Box 84,
Leeds LS1 4HU.

There were some who were naïve enough to believe that with the election of Margaret Thatcher there would be a more sympathetic response to women's issues. However, Thatcher's priorities would be determined by class and wealth and certainly not gender. Indeed, by 1982, Thatcher was to declare that, 'The battle for women's rights has been largely won.'[8] This was certainly not true for the working class woman. They, in particular, were affected by changes made by Thatcher's government to the Employment Protection Act, the abolition of the Fair Wages Resolution, and the reduction in the powers of the wages council. Working class women were also disproportionately affected by cuts in social security benefits and unemployment, reversing the progress made under the Equal Pay Act.

The writer Selma James said, 'I did not need Thatcher, although in some ways it was useful to show that a woman can be as much of a pig as a man.'[9]

One of the Christmas cards reminds us that for some – women and turkeys, in this case – Christmas has a negative side. For the women, invariably it means more hard work, and for turkeys, their demise.

Notes on Chapter 7

1. Michael Foot, quoted in *Who Said What When*, Bloomsburg, 1989.
2. Jim Callaghan, quoted in *Michael Foot* by Mervyn Jones, Victor Gollancz, 1994.
3. Neil Kinnock, quoted in *Tony Benn A Political Life* by David Russell, Continuum, London and New York, 2001.
4. Bob Dent, *Lessons of the General Strike*, Millenium, 1973.
5. Bob Dent, *Lessons of the General Strike*, Millenium, 1973.
6. Peter Pike MP, *Hansard*, 6 October 1985.
7. Ken Eastham MP, *Hansard*, 25 April 1987.
8. Margaret Thatcher, 26 July 1982, quoted in *Thatcher's Britain*, various authors, Pluto Press and New Socialist, 1983.
9. Selma James, interviewed by Cary Gee, *Tribune*, 31 October 2008.

CHAPTER 8

End of an Era

'I don't mind how much my ministers talk as long as they do what I say.'[1]

– Margaret Thatcher

Following her victory in 1987, Thatcher portrayed an image of even greater arrogance, coupled with one of invincibility. This twist on the Queen's Christmas broadcast sums up that feeling.

The role of other politicians, even in her Cabinet, was to serve and not question her. Little was she to know that, as Prime Minister, her time was limited and her 'servants', both in and out of the Cabinet, were soon to plot her downfall. Her election manifesto also contained the seeds of her own downfall – the Poll Tax. Almost from the first day of the new Parliament this issue was to dominate her final years in office, together with the Exchange Rate Mechanism (ERM).

The Poll Tax was based on the belief that the poorest among us should be subject to as much tax as the rich. Whether you were a 'duke or a dustman', you would pay a similar amount for your local services, with no account being taken of your personal circumstances.

Opposition within and even more so, outside Parliament, developed against the Poll Tax, including massive demonstrations and occasional violent clashes, with many ending in jail. The slogan 'Can't Pay, Won't Pay' was to become the rallying cry of many opposition groups. One card includes the date 1381, obviously evoking the spirit of the Peasants' Revolt, which in Essex at least, was triggered by successive Poll Taxes of 1377, 1379 and 1380. These earlier revolts widened to cover many other issues and although eventually failing, they created conditions which can be described as revolutionary. However, the revolt against the Poll Tax of the 1980s, where, once again, the poorest were expected to bear the greatest burden, was successful.

To scrap the Poll Tax was on the Christmas card wish list, together with some other issues to which we will refer.

Unemployment continued at a staggeringly high level and, in addition, the problem of inflation continued to cause concern. This Christmas card reflects the harsh times that were hitting some areas even more than others.

While unemployment increased, welfare benefits were still subject to cuts.

If we are to measure people by words alone, then in 1986 Thatcher became a friend of the earth. Warning that 'We might have begun ... a massive experiment with the system of the planet itself',[2] and on another occasion stating that '... it is mankind and its activities

Above: Artist: Maggie Guillon, devised by Trudy Begg.

Below left and right: Keighley Anti Poll Tax Union.

Right: Artist: Paul Morton, Leeds Postcards, PO Box 84, Leeds, LS1 4HU.

Below left: Artist Unknown.

Below right: Recycled Images.

Artist: Maggie Guillon, devised by Trudy Begg.

which are changing the environment of our planet in a damaging and dangerous way ... The evidence is there ... the damage is being done ...'[3] As Thatcher argued, 'the repair work needs to start without delay.'[4]

Sadly, the inactivity and deregulation of environmental control which had epitomised her years in office prior to 1988 continued in the years that followed, as she failed to back those fine words with action.

Her lack of positive action on environmental issues reflected the view she expressed at the time of the Falklands conflict, that 'It is good things like this war that helped to take people's minds off irrelevant issues like the environment'.[5]

This Christmas card arrives at a similar conclusion, with Thatcher and company 'dreaming of a green Christmas', but the angel on top of the tree, recognising that it was only a dream, 'yet another Christmas myth'.

The cuts in our public services continued.

Not surprisingly, her old enemy, the trade unions, had not disappeared. In 1988 came the dispute at P & O Ferries, where workers were sacked for refusing to sign contracts over a disagreement regarding working practices and safety issues.

One of Thatcher's later acts as Prime Minister was consistent with previous attempts to destroy the trade union movement; the obvious place for this was the docks, where the unions were well organised. This time her method was through privatisation of the Docks Labour Scheme, formed in 1949 by Ernest Bevin to prevent the hiring of casual labour. Hundreds of trade unionists were sacked, unlawfully as the Courts were later to rule. They did eventually receive compensation but, unfortunately, they were not allowed to return to work.

Top: Artist: Alan Hardman.

Middle: Printed by Economical Printers. Published by the South West TUC with thanks to Steve Bell.

Bottom: Published by the London Dockers Support Group, 22 Lassa Road, London SE9 6PU. Printed by Trade Union Printing Services Ltd, 30 Lime Street, Newcastle-Upon-Tyne NE1 2PQ.

Meanwhile, on the international front, Thatcher continued to oppose Mandela and the African National Congress which she viewed as a 'typical terrorist organisation'.[6] She also opposed sanctions, preferring instead a policy of so-called constructive engagement. The fact that this policy had failed dismally and the South African apartheid government was still entrenched in power seemed to have escaped her notice. While the government refused to act, many people around the world organised a boycott of South African goods.

Meanwhile, Thatcher held on to her belief in nuclear weapons and therefore acted as an obstruction to progress. The Christmas cards, once again, reflect the sender's opposition to the continued government support for their nuclear role, with the words 'countless individuals, commonly united to form one massive, unstoppable movement' – CND.

Another card painted by a 12-year-old child, Fatima, in the Bourj al Barajneh refugee camp in Lebanon illustrates what happened during the Gaza war and shows her compassion for the trauma faced by the children of Gaza. The translation reads, 'Oh children of Gaza, I came and I didn't find you.'

It is also appropriate that the next card, in a humorous way, highlights the discrimination against the limited role of women in one of the most important jobs, being on Santa's 'sleigh team'. Some would argue that being Prime Minister was an even more important form of employment. If it was, when Thatcher filled that position, she certainly did not see herself as a member of a team, but instead, **the** team.

Finally, the Tories ousted an increasingly hated Thatcher as leader. She resigned as Prime Minister. While not being naïve enough to imagine that one Tory, Thatcher, being replaced by another, Major, was a cause for celebration, there was still some satisfaction to be gleaned from the demise of someone who represented just about everything that socialists opposed.

Artist: Francis Boyle.

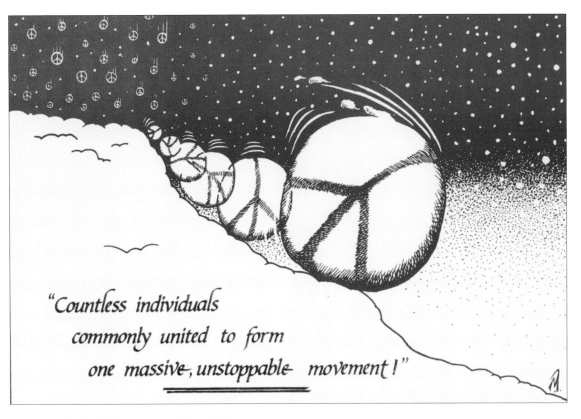

Artist: Paul Morton, printed by CND.

By Fatima (aged 12), Medical Aid for Palestinians (www.map.org.uk).

Left: Artist: Angela Martin, Leeds Postcards.

Right: Artist: Maggie Guillon, devised by Trudy Begg.

Notes on Chapter 8

1. Margaret Thatcher quoted in *Who Said What When*, Bloomsbury Publishing Ltd, London, 1989.
2. Margaret Thatcher, 27 September 1988, quoted in *How Green is Britain*, Friends of the Earth, Hutchinson Radius, 1990.
3. Margaret Thatcher, 8 November 1989, quoted in *How Green is Britain*, Friends of the Earth, Hutchinson Radius, 1990.
4. Friends of the Earth, *How Green is Britain*, Hutchinson Radius, 1990.
5. Margaret Thatcher, 1982, quoted in *Sound Bites*, New International Publications, Oxford, 1997.
6. Margaret Thatcher quoted in *Sound Bites*, New International Publications, 1997.

CHAPTER 9

Tories Continue Under Another Name and Leader

'They're all made out of ticky-tacky and they all look just the same.'[1]

– *Malvina Reynolds*

Following Thatcher's demise, John Major was elected by his parliamentary party as leader and therefore Prime Minister. He, like Thatcher, commenced his period in office with an equally insincere commitment: to a classless society.

While Major initially received the support of Thatcher, he was soon to discover that this would not last. It was appropriate that a Christmas card shows Thatcher returning to haunt Major while he was reading 'A Christmas Carol' by Charles Dickens, as she was a great admirer of the Victorian age. 'An age in which education rested on philanthropy and health care on charity. The absence of rights at work left employers free to exploit workers in appalling conditions. In which women knew their place and were denied the vote. In which class divisions were wide and unbridgeable.'[2]

Issues such as the Poll Tax, privatisation, low pay, unemployment and cuts in public services, including health, was Major's inheritance. Problems for which he was also responsible, as a member of the Cabinet in Thatcher's government.

His inheritance was not just in policies but also politicians and a public who seemed to have little faith in the government or the Labour leadership. A Christmas card shows them all 'up for sale' at 'bargain prices'.

One of the first issues Major had to deal with was the Poll Tax, which had been the main reason for Thatcher's 'reign' being brought to an end. Major admitted defeat with the abolition of this tax. The protests in Parliament had been considerable, but nothing compared with those in the streets. Another card highlights this issue.

One of Major's early innovations was the 'Citizens Charter', which was, supposedly, to assist in the improvement of public services. Also, greater regulation of the privatised utilities with increased competition. The Charter did not seem to have any positive impact and was seen by many as just another publicity stunt.

Far more important was the accusation in the Christmas card that the government was 'playing the race card'. That the 'new refugee policy will mean being deported to face torture and persecution. The immigration laws also seek to deny black people settled in the UK the right to family life, by not allowing families to be united in the UK. For those black people already here, the playing of the race card means an increase in racist attacks, as black people will be made scapegoats for unemployment and other failures of government policy ...'

Artist: Maggie Guillon, devised by Trudy Begg.

Artist: Maggie Guillon, devised by Trudy Begg.

Above left: Artist: Steve Bell, 1992.

Above right: Mike Nicholson. Published by NALGO 1 Mabledon Place, London WC1H 9AJ. Leeds Postcards PO Box 84, Leeds, England LS1 4HU.

Below: Artist: Maggie Guillon, devised by Trudy Begg.

Above: Artist: Maggie Guillon, devised by Trudy Begg.

Left: Cartoon: Dave Minto. West Midlands Anti-Deportation Campaign 101 Villa Road, Handsworth, Birmingham B19.

Printed and published by Chesterfield Unemployed Workers Centre. Artist: Maggie Guillon, devised by Trudy Begg.

To the surprise of many, Major won the General Election of 1992 and with it came the resignation of Neil Kinnock; he was replaced by John Smith as Leader of the Labour Party. As Neil had taken the party increasingly towards the 'right', the differences between them was not great.

One of Major's many failures was the Child Support Agency of 1992, being based on the belief that too many lone parents were being supported by the State, when too little, or nothing, was forthcoming on many occasions from the other parent. The Tories' attempt to rectify this was a disaster, as hundreds of thousands of lone parents failed to receive the needed financial support, or had to wait long periods of time to have their claims investigated. Often the investigations were botched.

Also in 1992, the TUC organised a mass "March for Jobs and Recovery", with many linking it to job losses in the mining industry.

While on the international front, loans to some of the poorest countries came with the burden of high interest rates often leaving the countries with massive debts.

Julius Nyere, Tanzanian President commenting on the International Monetary Fund, said, 'They ask me to make a choice between paying the debts of Tanzania and feeding the people of Tanzania. For me ... there is no moral choice.'[3] His people had to come first.

The cynicism is understandable; in 1961 President Kennedy explained that aid was a 'method by which the United States maintains a position of influence and control around the world and sustains a good many countries which would definitely collapse, or pass into the Communist bloc.'[4]

Above left: Tower Hamlet Miners Support Group.

Aabove right: Artist: Christine Smith; reproduced by kind permission of Wildcat Cards.

In 1994, Major was faced with a revolt over his decision to extend the scope of VAT on fuel, which, like the withdrawal from the ERM, was having a devastating effect on his popularity rating.

So great was the opposition to VAT on fuel that Labour, with a few abstentions and votes against by some Tories, inflicted their first significant defeat on the government since coming to power in 1979. This was immediately followed by an announcement to the House of Commons that they were withdrawing their proposals.

1994 did bring another piece of good news, with the end of the system of apartheid in South Africa. The ANC's demands, written into their 'Freedom Charter', as reflected in one of the cards, was about to be achieved, where 'South Africa belongs to all who live in it and that no government can justly claim authority unless it is based on the will of the people ... That only a democratic state, based on the will of the people, can secure to all, their birthright, without distinction of colour, race, sex or belief ...'[5]

Meanwhile, in the UK, public services were increasingly experiencing cuts in their budgets.

It was the most vulnerable who were most affected, as the Tory Government also continued their policy of cutting many State Benefits, including those for the disabled, by abolishing Invalidity Benefit, replacing it with the 'All Work Test'.

Above: Angela Martin, Leeds Postcards.

Below left: Artist: Anthony Evans, printed by Fingerprints (TU), Cardiff.

Below right: Artist: Maggie Guillon, devised by Trudy Begg.

" ... AND I BET THEY STILL BELIEVE IN FATHER CHRISTMAS! "

Crippen – Disabled Cartoonist. Printed by Freeways of London.

In 1994, the Tories passed the Criminal Justice and Public Order Act, which created a new range of offences, criminalising many more forms of peaceful protest.

The Act was subject to considerable opposition, particularly outside Parliament, where as George Monbiat notes, '... it succeeded in uniting all the disparate factions whose interests or activities it threatened ...'[6]

This Act was to be followed by others, which had similar intentions, including the Serious Organised Crime and Police Act in 1995 and the 1997 Protection from Harassment Act.

The Tory Government appeared to become increasingly concerned at the widening and more direct forms of protest, particularly road protests. Their reaction was not to respond positively to such protests, but instead to stifle them.

The campaigning organisation, Liberty, also protested against the Act, in particular in relation to trespassing assemblies. 'This gave the police the power to ban gatherings on either public or private land, which they "reasonably believe", could result in serious disruption. The breaking of this law could result in prison sentences or fines ...'[7]

Other environmental issues were being raised including polluted seas and the problems of low flying aircraft.

Meanwhile, scientists were concerned at their budget being cut by Major, and quoted back at him fears he also expressed in 1993, that '... perhaps we have undervalued science and the application of science in the United Kingdom over the past 20 to 30 years.'

Above left: SAS 136. South Atlantic Souvenirs.

Above right: SAS 140. South Atlantic Souvenirs.

Below: Artist: Jim Medway, Leeds Postcards.

Above: Artist: Kate Charlesworth.

Below left: Artist: Gillian Metcalfe for CND, Cymru.

Below right: Artist: Colin Wheeler.

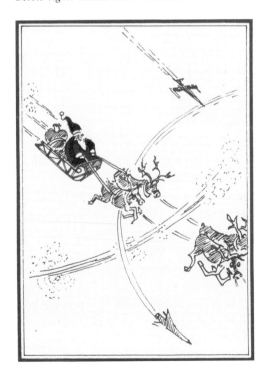

" . . . and we can save 700 lire by
not taking soil tests."

Inland Revenue Staff Federation, 23 Vauxhall Bridge Road, London SW1V 1EH.

One of the areas causing increasing concern was in the plans for the privatisation of the computer and secretarial work in the Inland Revenue. Opposition was not just about the philosophy of privatisation, or even how it would affect terms of employment, but the danger of 'information about you or your business getting into the wrong hands.'

Towards the end of Thatcher's term in office, a commitment was given to privatise the railways. This became a reality, but not during her term of office; instead it was John Major who was responsible for this in 1996, a year before being voted out of office. Yet we were told not to worry, as New Labour intended to return it to public ownership – a promise they never kept.

The privatisation programme from the 1980s to the present day not only concentrated wealth in fewer hands, but was also anti-democratic, transferring ownership, accountability and control from public representatives to a few major shareholders.

Also in the international sphere was the continuing worldwide campaign by Amnesty International 'to secure the release of prisoners of conscience, working for fair and prompt trials for all political prisoners and campaigns against torture and the death penalty.' The record of the Tories and New Labour in these areas has been appalling.

Another card highlights the work being carried out by the Terence Higgins Trust, leading campaigners to help those with HIV/Aids.

Meanwhile, not only were politicians subject to an increasing amount of criticism, but the Royal Family and its very institution was also under fire – or as one card put it 'one has been getting a very poor reception recently'.

Artist: Maggie Guillon, devised by Trudy Begg.

Artist: Francis Boyle.

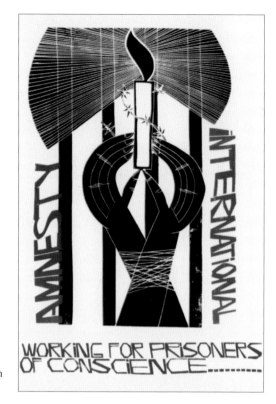

Right: Amnesty International.

Below: The Terence Higgins Trust, 52-54 Grays Inn Road, London WC1X 8JU.

Top: SAS 138. South Atlantic Souvenirs.

Middle and bottom: Artist: Alan Hardman.

Above and right: Artist: Maggie Guillon, devised by Trudy Begg.

That is not to imply that prior to this period the Royal Family had been free of criticism. Indeed, it's worth recalling the words of one of the great Englishmen, Tom Paine, who, in his book *The Rights of Man*, expressed the viewpoint that:

> Hereditary succession is a burlesque upon monarchy. It puts it in the most ridiculous light, by presenting it as an office which any child or idiot may fill. It requires some talent to be a common mechanic; but to be a king requires only the animal figure of man, a sort of breathing automaton.[8]

Prince Edward, who lives in a palace, receives a massive public income and owes his position in life to birth and not talent, declared that, 'We are forever being told that we have a rigid class structure. That's codswallop.'[9] If it is not 'rigid' and class bound, can he inform us how non-royals can join the club?

These Christmas cards reflected both the wish by many for a General Election and also the fear often felt that, after Labour's many defeats, history would repeat itself with another Tory victory. Because of his unpopularity, Major was to call the election at the last possible moment, but it was to no avail, with New Labour winning with a massive majority. There was the hope that this would bring an end to Tory policies, but sadly, they were often continued under New Labour.

Notes on Chapter 9

1. Malvina Reynolds, quoted in *Who Said What When*, Bloomsbury, 1989.
2. *Thatcher's Britain*, various authors, Pluto Press, 1983.
3. Julius Nyerere, quoted in *Fight Against Poverty*, Fight World Poverty Lobby, 1986.
4. President Kennedy, 1961, quoted in *The Creation of World Poverty* by Teresa Hayter, Pluto Press, 1985.
5. African National Congress, 'Freedom Charter', quoted in *Apartheid* by Donald Woods and Mike Bostock.
6. George Monbiot, *Times Literary Supplement*, 21 February 1997.
7. 'Liberty', quoted in George Monbiot, *Times Literary Supplement*, 21 February 1997.
8. Tom Paine, *The Rights of Man*, Everyman's Library, 1993.
9. Prince Edward, *The Observer Magazine*, 9 November 2008.

CHAPTER 10

New Labour –
Old Tory Values

'The Labour Party must have as its aim the establishment of a socialist society, otherwise it will have no significance in the life of the nation.'[1]

– Aneurin Bevan

Tony Blair was elected as Labour – or as he declared – New Labour Leader in 1994.

While extending to the members his 'Best Wishes for Christmas and the New Year', this was as far as his festive spirit extended. Instead of embarking on that spirit of 'giving', he decided to 'take', or indeed 'steal' from the membership, their Labour Party, while treating their history as irrelevant. Both the party and its history were, like some Christmas presents, rejected, as was Nye's advice. New Labour was to incorporate an entirely new set of values, alien to so many who had over the generations been attracted to the Movement. For them, Labour and Socialism were to be the past.

Nye, in his resignation from the Cabinet in 1951, also explained, or warned, how those core values often change, stating in a parliamentary speech that:

Those who lived their lives in mountainous and rugged countries are always afraid of avalanche, and they know that avalanches start with the movement of a very small stone. First, the stone starts on a ridge between two valleys – one valley desolate and the other valley populace. The pebble starts, but nobody bothers about the pebble, until it gains way, and soon the whole valley is overwhelmed. That is how the avalanche starts, that is the logic of the present situation ...[2]

Yet the changes Blair immediately introduced on becoming Labour Leader and later, Prime Minister, did not start with the political equivalent of a 'pebble', but with the 'avalanche'. The effect of that 'avalanche' was felt immediately and continues to this present day.

Those values and ideas which had been fought for and passed down over the centuries by the early pioneers were seen by New Labour as irrelevant, or as portrayed in the Christmas card, a 'burden' which will 'soon be lifted'.

The values incorporated in this card were to be unceremoniously dumped, having no relevance to the Thatcherite party Blair was moulding. One of the first changes was to scrap Clause IV, removing it from the Labour Party constitution, which Tony Benn declared was equivalent to removing the 'crucifixes out of the church'.[3] Embedded in this clause was so much of what Labour represented including a commitment to the redistribution of wealth, and support for public services and industries, with decisions

Left: Artist: Maggie Guillon, devised by Trudy Begg.

Below: Published by the late Alex Falconer.

Published by the late Alex Falconer.

affecting them not being left to a few financiers, but workers also having a role in this process.

After eighteen years of Tory government, it was obvious to Blair that the party would accept these changes, as they were desperate to see the return of a Labour government. They were also concerned that opposition to it would project an image of disunity which may damage Labour's chances. Some believed that New Labour would deliver the good life. Others convinced themselves that once they were returned to government, the issues would be quietly dropped and Labour would return to its traditional values.

As some argued, this was to misjudge seriously what was happening to the Labour Party and the dramatic move to the right to which Blair and others were taking it. If some Labour members were confused, or unsure as to the extent of the change, Mrs Thatcher was not, announcing in Parliament, that, '... I see a lot of socialism behind their front bench, but not in Mr Blair ...'[4]

In later years, others were to go further, such as Geoffrey Howe, commenting on Thatcher, 'Her real triumph was to have transformed not just one party, but two, so that when Labour did eventually return, the great bulk of Thatcherism was accepted as irreversible.'[5]

With New Labour forming the government in 1997, Blair, Brown and others immediately began to build on and implement the plans they had formed when in Opposition.

Their decision to confine Clause IV to the dustbin of history was a signal that the ideals and policies associated with it would experience a similar fate. Instead, 'market forces' summed up much of what New Labour was all about, thereby accepting Thatcher's claim that there was 'no alternative.'[6]

Artist: Maggie Guillon, devised by Trudy Begg.

Artist: Maggie Guillon, devised by Trudy Begg.

Artist: Maggie Guillon, devised by Trudy Begg.

To highlight Blair's, and in later years Brown's, attachment to Thatcher and Thatcherism, they invited her back for a visit to No. 10. The fact that she was hated by the Labour Movement was irrelevant to them. Blair even 'lauded her as 'a radical, not a Tory'.[7]

While Thatcher had lost faith in Major to carry on her politics, as already emphasised, she did not have similar doubts about Blair. This is reflected in one of the cards which replaces the traditional nativity scene of Mary holding Baby Jesus, with Thatcher cuddling a 'Baby' Blair reading him a bedtime story entitled 'How to Grind the Workers Down'.

They commenced and continued through their periods in office to prove their right-wing views, by discarding the belief which traditionally disassociated Labour from the Tories and was an integral part of Clause IV, namely, the redistribution of wealth.

Throughout his long term in office, Blair was to show time and again his opposition to the redistribution of wealth and income. When, as Prime Minister, he was interviewed by Jeremy Paxman who asked him whether 'an individual can earn too much money?' Blair replied, 'I don't really...' Paxman also asked Blair, on approximately eight occasions, the linked question of whether 'it is acceptable for the gap between rich and poor to widen?'[8] Blair continually refused to answer this question, the answer to which generations of socialists had taken for granted, that is, the commitment to the redistribution of wealth in favour of the poor.

As Blair had shown himself to be totally disinterested in traditional Labour values, his refusal to answer this question is curious. Mandelson had no such problem, declaring on another occasion that '... we are intensely relaxed about people getting filthy rich.'[9] Even more inappropriate, at the time of the banking crisis in 2010 and the obscene bonuses handed out to the bankers, Mandelson was to proclaim 'haven't the rich suffered enough?'[10]

When Thatcher and the Tories came to power in 1979, they began to redistribute wealth, but, sadly, in favour of those who already had considerable amounts of money. One of the ways they did this was to reduce the top rate of tax from 60 to 40 per cent, and also introduce a national insurance ceiling.

Instead of reversing these policies, when New Labour came to power, they decided instead to further tip the scales in favour of the rich by implementing even more tax cuts for them.

Furthermore, the New Labour Government, although subject to rebellions in Parliament, almost immediately began to attack the benefits of some of the most vulnerable, including lone parents and the disabled. Like so many other aspects of their policies, they were emulating the Tories.

Another group that was to feel the effects of New Labour cuts was young people wishing to enter into higher education; New Labour introduced tuition and top-up fees. New Labour argued that they could no longer find the money to finance higher education, as had been done even under the Tories. Who would have thought that a Labour government would end free higher education? The answer was a New Labour, not Labour government, with totally different values. Once again, there were rebellions in Parliament, but these and student protests were ignored.

Yet they still managed to raise the money to finance the rich even more through the tax system: to fight wars, and later, to bail out the banks while announcing their intention to replace Trident. New Labour showed that it was not a shortage of money that was the problem, but a shortage of socialist ideals.

Above left: Artist: Alan Hardman.

Above right: © Biff Products BCM Biff, London WC1N 3XX.

Another way of reducing inequality is through increased investment in the public services, on which more deprived communities are particularly dependent. Yet, in the first two years, the New Labour Government decided to link its public expenditure plans to those of the previous Tory administration. Services which had been experiencing cuts were initially to experience a similar situation with the election of New Labour.

On the positive side, the Minimum Wage was introduced, which Keir Hardie had campaigned for approximately a century earlier. Yet to make a major impact on the redistribution of incomes, it needed to have been set at a much higher level and there was no evidence of this happening.

 The other aspect of Clause IV which Blair rejected was support for the public services and industries. Once again, he decided to build on the Thatcher legacy of privatisation, rather than what he promised in opposition, of supporting the public bodies. This massive privatisation programme was shown in many of the Christmas cards of that period.

That 'pretty straight sort of guy',[11] as Tony Blair once described himself, appeared to commit the Party to, among other things, a publicly owned and publicly accountable railway system under a Labour government. Indeed, his Deputy Leader, John Prescott, bluntly stated that any privatisation of the railway system will be reversed and the industry 'will be returned to public ownership'.[12] Yet they failed to keep this promise.

Artist: Maggie Guillon, devised by Trudy Begg.

Artist: Alan Hardman.

Produced by the CWU Critchley Fighting Fund.

New Labour was also to legislate for a referendum to gain agreement to set up a Welsh Assembly. The 'Yes' campaign was supported by tens of millions of pounds of government money; promotional leaflets were delivered to every household from the government and the media remained compliant.

Some warned that the Assembly was the first step towards a separatist Wales; yet we were told that an Assembly would kill off the nationalists (also in Scotland), when in fact the Welsh Nationalists later joined in a coalition government with New Labour. The nationalists who went on to share power with New Labour are of the same party which was born out of a hatred of the English and the Jews. Its first leader, Saunders Lewis, was a great admirer of Hitler. Commenting on the latter, he argued that, '... English opinion, which had for years been strongly in support of Germany, was entirely turned against her. The Welsh followed like sheep through a gap.'[13] He also opposed English children being evacuated into Wales, declaring that they would 'completely submerge and destroy all of Welsh national tradition ...' For Lewis, this 'movement of population is one of the most terrible threats to the continuation and to the life of the Welsh Nation, that has ever been suggested in history.'[14]

So while the nationalists and seemingly some in New Labour were working for a separatist Wales, others, like the late Leo Abse, once pointed out that as socialists we 'marched under the banner in Wales, calling on the workers of the world to unite. I certainly do not intend ... at this stage in my political life, to spend my time calling on the workers in Scotland, England and Wales to disunite ...'[15] Nye Bevan also shared those sentiments.

The strike at Critchley Labels, lasting for over two years, followed redundancies announced at the plant and a refusal, to 'reinstate members, or improve redundancy payments, or even maintain their agreement with CWU to consult in the future on staffing matters.'

Artist: Maggie Guillon, devised by Trudy Begg.

Artist: Maggie Guillon, devised by Trudy Begg.

With best wishes

Tim CARSTAIRS

Have a Happy Christmas from all at MAG

Humanitarian Mine Action MAG Mines Advisory Group. www.mag.org.uk.

ASBOs were introduced shortly after the election of New Labour, with the intention of clamping down on 'yob culture'. They seemed to have been welcomed by many confronted by this behaviour, while others had their objections to them. Also there was the problem that approximately 50 per cent of these orders were breached

Sexual discrimination was a problem demanding change. The government did in fact repeal Section 28 of the Local Government Act and other legislation relating to discrimination against same sex couples.

The government also signed the Ottawa Convention and later passed the UK Anti-personnel Landmine Act in 1998. The banning of anti-personnel landmines was mainly a victory for those who had conducted such an effective campaign on this issue. We are still living with the legacy of those landmines, with people still being killed every day in places like Angola and Afghanistan

As highlighted by the Christmas cards in this book, there has been opposition to nuclear weapons since their inception. This opposition has taken many forms and one which attracted attention was in 1999, when three Trident Ploughshare activists – Ullar Roder, Ellen Moxley and Angie Zelter – 'boarded the Trident research barge and cleared out its laboratory, throwing computers and other equipment in the deep waters of the Loch Goil. They then sat down to take a picnic and watch the beautiful sunset.'

At the trial, Sheriff Margaret Gimblett acquitted them of all charges on the grounds that their action was justified, since Trident presented an active threat that was illegal under international law.

Sarah Isaacs Parliamentay Worker CND Cymru Bridgend Cottage
Llangamarch Powys LD4 4ED tel 01591 620561

Illegality of Trident.

On Thursday 21 October this year Sheriff Margaret Gimbley instructed a jury at Greenock Sheriff Court to acquit three women who had caused £80 000 damage to a Trident related 'acoustic research barge' during a Trident Ploughshares 2000 disarmament action.

Sheriff Margaret Gimblett said 'I have to conclude that the three accused ......were justified in thinking that Great Britain in their use of Trident, not simply possession, the use and deployment of Trident allied with that use and deployment at times of great unrest, coupled with its first use policy and in the absence of indication from any government official then or now that such a use fell into any strict category suggested in the ICJ opinion.....the threat or use of Trident could be construed as a threat, indeed has been construed by others as a threat and as such is an infringement of international and customary law.'

To summarise :**To threaten with nuclear weapons is unlawful.** Please urge the British Government to stop breaking the law.

The next decade is a **decade for a culture of peace and violence for the children of the world**. Please continue to do all you can to help get rid of weapons of mass destruction. Thank you for all your hard work in the past. *Have a peaceful and Happy New Year.* *Best wishes,*

Sarah

Sarah Isaacs CND Cymru.

The Trident Three

Above: Sarah Isaacs, CND Cymru – Trident Ploughshares.

Above right: Design by Johanna Berkin – Trident Ploughshares 42-46 Bethel Street, Norwich, Norfolk NR2 1NR. http://www.gn.apc.org/tp2000/.

Right: Heathrow Association for the Control of Aircraft Noise. www.hacan.org.uk.

Another environmental threat was the possible third runway at Heathrow airport. This Christmas card reflects the concerns and opposition to night time flying and the noise it brings with it at Heathrow, together with the increased emissions. This and related issues were to be continued over the next decade, with the decision of the government in favour of a third runway. It is interesting to note that although this card was published soon after the election of New Labour, these campaigners had already recognised that they 'govern, not for the people, but on behalf of big business ...' They also recognised that in New Labour's decision-making, 'the environment is ignored'.

Cover: Chris Duggan duggan.illustrated@dsl.pipex.com for Parliamentary Brief www.thepolitician.org.

Artist: Stuart Ritchie; published by the late Alex Falconer, MEP.

Printed and published by MSF Centre, 33-37
Moreland Street, London EC1V 8HA.

This Christmas card seems to imply that Blair's belief in the need to immediately join the Euro triumphed over Brown's opposition. While it might have seemed like this at the time, the reality was to be totally different. At the time of writing, Britain is not and does not seem likely in the foreseeable future, to become a part of the Euro zone

Still on the subject of the European Union, fellow MEP, the late Alex Falconer, put his experiences of New Labour and the Tories, from 1984 to 1999, in the form of a Christmas card.

The issue of women and equality, or lack of equality, recurs in Christmas cards welcoming the decision of the government to introduce, in 1999, the 'right for parents to take 13 weeks parental leave as required by the EU Parental Leave Directive. However, under pressure from the CBI, the UK Government has arbitrarily excluded all parents of children born before 15 December 1999.' The other theme which runs through these Christmas cards, in the period of New Labour, is their willingness to put the wishes of employers before the employees. Other cards relating to women's' issues are also depicted.

Another issue, which was to dominate much of the news, was the £755 million Millenium Dome, which turned out to be as meaningless and devoid of sound ideas as New Labour.

Realising that in creating what was in reality a new party, New Labour, lacking any real socialist beliefs, had to put in place new systems, which would dramatically weaken, if not wipe out the 'left' from elected office. This included almost every level of decision-making for the election of New Labour candidates, including the European Parliament, House of Commons, Scottish Parliament and Welsh Assembly.

Their one failure was Ken Livingstone, who, although originally prevented from being Labour's candidate for the position of Mayor of London, successfully stood instead as an Independent. He later rejoined New Labour and won the election to be re-elected as Mayor.

Artists: Maggie Guillon and Trudy Begg, Humbug Cards.

Artist: Stuart L Ritchie; published by the late Alex Falconer, MEP.

"Sorry, the Blairs have sold out."

Above: Humbug Cards. Artist: Maggie Guillon, devised by Trudy Begg.

Right: Artist: Steve Smith.

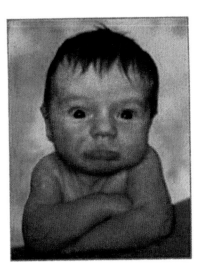

I don't care what Mummy said!

I want a <u>new</u> Labour government, peace on earth, goodwill towards men, women and dumb animals, a nuclear free world and a greener, healthier environment. Also, an end to Third World debt and an end to the Capitalist exploitation of the masses.

Humbug Cards.
Artist: Maggie
Guillon, devised
by Trudy Begg.

The electorate also shared their disappointment, with less than 60 per cent bothering to vote in the General Election, which was one of the lowest turnouts since the end of the Second World War.

As at other times of Blair's premiership, there were even more Christmas cards from those involved in the wider Labour Movement, who were totally disillusioned with him and New Labour. These also included those who had, at the beginning of his term in office, sent cards expressing their confidence in him. Others were not disillusioned, having had no confidence in New Labour from the outset. Having been brought up in a Tory family and married into a Labour one, Blair remained loyal to his own family's views, and merely gave it a new name, New Labour.

Notes on Chapter 10

1. Aneurin Bevan, *My Life with Nye*, Jennie Lee, Jonathan Cape, 1980.
2. Aneurin Bevan, *Hansard* Volume 487, 1951.
3. Tony Benn, *Free at Last, Tony Benn Diaries, 1991-2001*, Arrow Books, 2002.
4. Mrs Thatcher, quoted in *The Independent*, 28 May 1995.
5. Geoffrey Howe, BBC, 13 October 2005.
6. Margaret Thatcher in http://en.wikipedia.org/wiki/there-is-noalternative
7. *The Guardian*, 3 September 2010.
8. Tony Blair interviewed by Jeremy Paxman, Newsnight, BBC.
9. Peter Mandelson, *Financial Times*, 23 October 1998.
10. *The Guardian*, 17 December 2010.
11. Tony Blair, referred to in *The Vote* by Paul Foot, Penguin, 2005.
12. John Prescott, referred to in *The Vote* by Paul Foot, Penguin, 2005.
13. Saunders Lewis, 'Y Ddraig Goch', June 1933.
14. Saunders Lewis, *The Welsh Nationalist Party 1925-1945. A Call to Nationhood*, University of Wales Press, 1983. Dr Hywel Davies quoting from 'Ddraig Goch', November 1938.
15. Leo Abse, *Hansard*, 16 December 1976.

CHAPTER 11

No Ethics, Just Blair's New Labour

'Our foreign policy must have an ethical dimension and must support the demands of other people for the democratic right on which we insist ourselves. The Labour Government will put human rights at the heart of our foreign policy.'[1]

– Robin Cook, Foreign Secretary

Blair's second term in office was to be dominated by the unethical and illegal war in Iraq, although he wished to project a different message. He attempted, as the card shows, to emphasise what he saw as New Labour successes.

One hundred and fifty Labour MPs rebelled in a parliamentary vote, in the hope of preventing this war. There was even greater opposition to the war outside of Parliament, including massive demonstrations, up to two million strong. Yet Blair, Brown, the Cabinet and the majority of MPs still treated the opposition to the war with contempt, preferring to protect their own careers before that of the Iraqi people. Hundreds of thousands of people have lost their lives in the conflict.

Many were aware that there was no ethical dimension to the war; the intention was to obtain control of the region and Iraqi oil – for power and profits. We were wrongly informed that the war was legal and that Iraq had weapons of mass destruction that could be used within forty-five minutes, posing a grave threat to world peace.

Having heard Blair's statement, the words of Jonathan Swift come to mind:

Falsehood flies and truth comes limping after it: so that when men come to be understood, it is too late, the jest is over and the tale has had its effect. [2]

After Blair and Brown had been found out, a new set of excuses were served up to justify the war, including the so-called fight for liberty, democracy, human rights, together with defence of the Marsh Arabs.

When even these arguments failed to convince, some were left to explain the war as a response to the attacks by Saddam Hussain on the World Trade Centre. The fact that there was no evidence to justify this claim, even by the USA's own secret service, did not prevent it from being used as a defence for the war. The cry went out 'Stop the War' while another card portrays a massive anti-war demonstration. The horrors of the war with the torture of Iraqis by American soldiers at Abu Ghraib prison at a later date are also highlighted.

Above left: Cartoon by Dros. Published by Labour Left Briefing PO Box 2378 London E5 9QU. Printed by Wernhams Printers Ltd (TU) 4 Forster Road, London N17.

Above right: Published by The Labour Party, Millbank Tower, London SW1P 4GT. Printed by Dorling Print Ltd, Dorling House, 44 Wates Way, Mitcham, Surrey CR4 4HR.

Below: Photograph by Thomas Clayton. Design by Jan Byrne. www.stopwar.org.uk.

Right: Artist: Alan Hardman.

Below: Iran; Maryam Rajavi.

As the world celebrates the advent of the New Year and the birth of Jesus Christ, the messenger of peace and compassion, I offer my best wishes for a joyful and successful year to you and your family.
It is my conviction that the time for celebration and happiness for my fellow compatriots will arrive when the religious tyranny in Iran is overthrown.

Maryam Rajavi

As these and other Christmas cards highlighted in this book show, we have been in violent conflict with Iraq for the past century. Invariably the reason for such conflict has been control and ownership of Iraqi oil – the second biggest oil field in the world.

Yet at the time of the long war in the 1980s between Iraq and Iran, the former was regarded as our friend and the latter the enemy. Although the terms 'friends' and 'enemies' had limitations in this instance. The USA supplied Iran and the Tory Government had sold dual-use equipment to Saddam.

Iran is once again the 'enemy' because of its links with and support for the Palestinians, Hezbollah in the Lebanon, and also the claims that it is producing nuclear weapons. Yet even if the charge can be supported, how can New Labour criticise them, when we too have nuclear weapons and have made no criticism of Israel's long-standing ownership of such weapons? To make these points is not to support the regime in Iran, but merely to highlight the weakness and hypocrisy of the New Labour Government.

The previous Christmas card highlights the opposition to the Iranian Government.

Still on the subject of foreign policy, with the re-election of New Labour, it was 'business as usual' in their response to the continuing conflict between Israel and Palestine.

As 'War on Want' reminded us in 2008, 'The creation of the State of Israel 60 years ago, was a catastrophic event, not only for the thousands of Palestinians who were killed, but also for the millions who still live in poverty as refugees around the region. Palestinian misery increased in 1967 when Israel took military control of the West Bank [including East Jerusalem] and Gaza. This continuing occupation, along with the illegal Separation Wall, has destroyed any semblance of a Palestinian economy. Today, 70% of people in the Occupied Palestinian Territories live in crushing poverty, and more than half rely on food aid to survive ... The UK has continued to support Israel with trade preferences and arms sales, irrespective of its treatment of the Palestinian people.'[3]

The depth of the problem and the hypocrisy of countries like the UK and the USA go even deeper. For Israel also has its own nuclear weapons and is the only ocountry in the Middle East to have them. Yet they are never subject to criticism from New Labour, or the representatives of other Western states, while Iran, with no evidence of such weapons, but

IS THAT THE STAR OF BETHLEHEM OR ANOTHER ISRAELI MISSILE?

Artist: Ken Sprague. © Leeds Postcards, 4 Granby Rd, Leeds LS6 3AS.

Right: Campaign to Free Vanunu and for a Nuclear Free Middle East. 185 New Kent Road, London SE1 4AG.

Below: World Development Movement, 25 Beehive Place, London SW9 7QR.

supposedly attempting to develop them, is seen as a threat to the Middle East and a part of what the then US President George W Bush called the 'axis of evil'.

Evidence of Israel's nuclear arsenal was exposed by Mordecai Vanunu, a former nuclear technician. For telling the truth, he was jailed for eighteen years, the majority of them in solitary confinement at Shikma prison. On his release in 2004, he declared that 'my message today to the world is: open the Dimond reactor for inspections.'[4] He also added his support for all nuclear weapons worldwide, not just Israel's, to be dismantled. Yet after being released from one prison, he was subject to another form of imprisonment; a refusal to be allowed to leave the country or to speak to journalists – a form of internal exile. The New Labour Government remained silent on his imprisonment, as they too often did on Israeli atrocities against the Palestinians.

Still on the subject of our foreign policy is the issue of world poverty. As we waste money on weapons of war and wars throughout the world, the cry still goes out, 'No More Hungry People'. Sadly, the leaders of the world, who could rectify this wrong, are not listening, or they don't care. It is so wrong that the future of the world's poor should increasingly be determined by the amount in charity collection boxes. Oxfam reported in 2006 that for every £1 that the world spends on Aid, £15 goes on arms. In total £561 billion a year was spent on arms.

Meanwhile, after more than fifty years of cruel opposition from the United States Government, the Cuban revolution still survives.

The Embassy of the

Republic of Cuba

sends you

Best Wishes

for the forthcoming year

Cuban Embassy.

Above: Design and print by Classic Grafix.

Right: © HAS/Doughnut Design. Hunt Saboteurs Association PO Box 2786 Brighton BN2 2AX. www.huntsabs.org.uk.

AMICUS the Union: www.amicustheunion.org.

In the constituency of Blaenau Gwent, the steel plant, which had at one time employed 12,000, was to close. A brave fight opposing the closure by the trade unions was to no avail; they were faced with an incompetent management whose decision was based on greed. Many of the management and board of directors responsible for the destruction of the plant resigned, yet still received massive pay-outs and pensions. For the majority of the workforce, their future was less rosy, with the dole queue or a low-paid job awaiting them.

The welfare of animals, with the issue of hunting with dogs, was to become a major parliamentary issue. One MP, who quoted Doctor Stanley Johnson, said that 'It is very strange and very melancholy, that the paucity of human pleasure should persuade us ever, to call hunting one of them.'[5]

The government was called upon to 'Tally no more' and support a ban on this activity. After much dithering by the government many back bench MPs forced the issue, resulting in a ban, which the Tories were committed to repeal when they are next returned to office.

The Christmas card from the trade union Amicus is a reminder that 'The gender pay gap in the UK remains unacceptably wide at 18.4%'. And that 'Compulsory equal pay reviews are the only way to make certain that employers have an equality-proofed pay system and that women get the reward they deserve for the work they do.'

Meanwhile, there is another Christmas card from those demanding equal parenting rights and how the 'defective family court system' highlights this. In order to bring their

We remind you about the very many
children who will again not see
good parents and
grandparents at Xmas
because of our defective family
court system.

We know that many are working
hard to remedy this, and we thank
those that are.

We hope that you have a
wonderful Xmas with your
children - and think of those who
are not so lucky.

Equal Parenting Council
www.EqualParenting.org

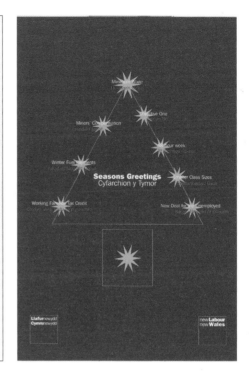

Above left: Equal Parenting Campaign. www.equalparenting.org.

Above right: Promoted by Matt Carter, General Secretary, the Labour Party. Printed by The Production House.

grievances to the attention of the public and the government, Fathers 4 Justice were, and continue to be, involved in a number of high profile stunts.

Once again New Labour attempts to highlight their achievements.

Finally, the membership of New Labour continued to collapse, following the war in Iraq and the rejection of so many Labour values.

Notes on Chapter 11

1. Robin Cook, Press Conference on becoming Foreign Secretary, 12 May 1997.
2. Jonathan Swift, *The Examiner*, 9 October 1710.
3. 'Up Front Sixty Years', 'War on Want', 2008.
4. Modicai Vanunu, after emerging from Shikma Prison, 21 April 2004.
5. Tony Banks in a Parliamentary address quotes the Poet and Essayist, Dr Stanley Johnson, in 'An Anecdote of Stanley Johnson'.

CHAPTER 12

Blair's Third and Final Term

'The ideas of socialism and democracy, like liberty, equality and fraternity, came into the world joined together and woe to those who would put them asunder.'[1]
– *Michael Foot*

Blair, commencing his third term in office, seemed as Thatcher did in the same period of her premiership, increasingly arrogant and disdainful of opinion other than his own. In the third term, they also shared the experience of rejection, leading to their respective resignations as Prime Minister.

With the defeat of the Tories, led by Michael Howard, David Cameron was elected leader of what had become known as the 'nasty party', as described by its then Party Chairwoman Theresa May MP. Cameron immediately started to re-brand the party, using more moderate language, while attempting to be seen to be the friend of everyone, from the down-trodden to the super rich, the environmentalists and the polluters, the libertarians and the clamp-down brigade, but always under the guise of someone with a social conscience. He seemed to be attempting to become Tony Blair Mark II, at a time when the people were beginning to reject Blairism.

Meanwhile, with a few exceptions, the politics of the Tories did not change significantly. The right was still with us and who better to put them forward than old Etonian Cameron – a former member of the infamous Bullingdon Club. Although, to be fair to Cameron, he did not regard being an old Etonian as a drawback to understanding the plight of the 'have nots'. Indeed, he was to declare that 'I don't buy these class things, because they're all going.'[2] An announcement that one of the bastions of the class system, Eton, was also 'going' did not come.

Internationally, the war in Iraq and increasingly Afghanistan continued to rage, thanks to the support of the USA and the UK governments, even though so many civilians and soldiers continued to be killed.

Meanwhile, the New Labour government continued to support Israel, even to the extent of selling them military equipment, which could be used against the Palestinian people. Israel also continues to receive massive financial support and arms from the USA. Both the USA and Britain are willing to sell arms to many repressive regimes throughout the world.

There seems little doubt that New Labour policies and wars in the Middle East have increased terrorism worldwide. The government used this as an excuse to tighten up the laws, including the introduction of powers to detain suspects for twenty-eight days without charge.

Artist: Martin Rowson.

Artist: Martin Rowson 2002. A
Red Pepper Production. www.
redpepper.org.uk.

Artist: Polyp; www.polyp@polyp.
org.uk.

The 28 Days of Christmas?

Liberty, 21 Tabard Street, London SE1 4LA. www.liberty-human-rights.org.uk.

Innocent people are also getting involved, with the Brazilian electrician Jean Charles de Menezes being unlawfully killed in the days following the terrorist explosions in London in 2005, when members of the police anti-terrorist squad and Special Forces claimed to have mistakenly thought he was a terrorist on the loose. A card shows how innocent people are being caught up in the war on terror.

In the UK, owing to the growing number of cancer patients, Parliament passed legislation banning smoking in public places, which came into force in 2007.

Another health issue was the decision to allow licensed pubs and clubs to open twenty-four hours a day. This concerned many, partly because of the potential increase in illness, such as liver disease, and also an increase in violence.

On the subject of race, or skin colour, one card featured the birth of Jesus and questioned the assumption that Jesus would be white.

One of the rare but important successes of the government was the agreement between various groups and political parties to set up the Assembly in Northern Ireland. While conflict continues, it is now, thankfully, at a much lower level and the Assembly is up and running.

Unfortunately, a similar card was not produced by the Unionists regarding the setting up of the Assembly.

The conflict arising from disagreement as to when Blair should resign as PM and Leader of the Labour Party increasingly dominated the media and the party's standing in the opinion polls. This debate had nothing to do with ideas, with the direction the party should go, but mainly the career prospects of two individuals: Brown and Blair.

What also came over was the arrogance of Brown, who obviously assumed that the position of leader was his prerogative, although he did not have the courage to contest the position with the death of John Smith. Also the arrogance of Blair, who supposedly agreed with Brown the date of his departure, with the latter becoming the new leader. They both epitomised all that was wrong with New Labour.

For others, their Christmas wish, shown in one of the cards, was for 'a Blair free New Year'. No doubt, it reflected a desire to return to the Socialist ideas which first attracted them to the Labour Movement; Brown may have shared their wish – but perhaps for less noble reasons.

T-shirt design by Vivienne Westwood for Liberty. Photograph by Cindy Palmano.

Humbug Cards. Artist: Maggie Guillon, devised by Trudy Begg.

Humbug Cards. Artist: Maggie Guillon, devised by Trudy Begg.

Humbug Cards. Artist: Maggie Guillon, devised by Trudy Begg.

Above left: Designed and produced by Maureen and Maureen.

Above right: Artist: Martin Rowson for the Parliamentary Press Gallery, House of Commons; www.parliamentarypressgallery.org.uk.

Below: Artist: Martin Rowson.

Left: Artist: Christine Hankinson, Leeds Postcards.

Above: Designed by Cathie Shuttleworth for Oxfam.

Since retirement, much of Blair's time has been spent in making a considerable amount of money through his directorships, lectures, company and for writing his autobiography. As John Pilger suggests, 'Who wants to be a millionaire?' is 'the song Tony hums every morning when he rises and tots up his latest windfall ...'[3] Perhaps his answer to that question is, 'I do', but Cherie is sure to join in the chorus, with the words, 'we do, we are, many times over.' On occasions like this, the words on the Christmas card of Mahatma Ghandi springs to mind, 'The World has enough for every man's need, but not enough for every man's greed.'

Notes on Chapter 12

1. Michael Foot MP, *People for the People*, edited by David Rubenstein, Ithaca Press, London, 1973.
2. David Cameron, *Observer Magazine*, 9 November 2008.
3. John Pilger, *The Guardian – The Guide*, 9 February 2008.

CHAPTER 13

Another New Labour Leader – Tory Values Continue

'It is easier to rob, by setting up a bank, than hold up a bank clerk.'[1]

– Berthold Brecht

Although Brown, together with Blair, was one of the most important architects of New Labour, he seemingly liked to foster the impression that he was still not a part of it; given the opportunity, this would become increasingly obvious. He was portrayed as someone whose roots were still in the old Labour Party and indeed a man of the people.

Those who were naïve enough to believe that Brown would return to his and the party's socialist roots were to be bitterly disappointed. In the most visual way, he deliberately sent out the message that it was to be business as usual, by inviting Thatcher to No. 10 Downing Street, as Blair did before him. Seeing them together was a reminder of the words in George Orwell's *Animal Farm*, that 'the creatures outside looked from pig to man and from man to pig and from pig to man again; but already it was impossible to say which was which.'

Brown also appointed into Government Digby Jones, the former head of the employers' union, the CBI. This man described the trade unions as an 'irrelevance. They are backward-looking and not on today's agenda.'[3] Could Brown not appreciate the irony of appointing as a minister someone who viewed with such disdain the organisation responsible for the birth of the Labour Party? Jones was soon to resign his ministerial position and revert to type by attacking the government.

Quite ironically, Thatcher's visit to No. 10 coincided with the day Northern Rock collapsed. Both the visit and the collapse should have been a reminder to us all of their respective roles and faith in market forces, bankers, financiers and the deregulation of the financial institutions. Did they not understand that if you deregulate the banking system, leaving their direction to the 'invisible hand' of market forces, then they are accountable to no-one, with politicians being an irrelevance? With the deregulation, we were left with powerless politicians, only interested in their re-election, and corrupt and incompetent bankers, only interested in their bonuses. Meanwhile, the economy was on the verge of collapse and millions were destined for the dole queue.

A lot of these problems could have been avoided if he had acted on past warnings about the banking sector and capitalism.

The warning came from one of the most prominent of economists, John Maynard Keynes, when he observed that 'Capitalism is the extraordinary belief that the nastiest of men for the nastiest of motives, will somehow work for the benefit of all.'[4] Or back

Above left: Artist: Martin Rowson.

Above right: Cartoon by Polyp. War on Want, Development House, 56-64 Leonard Street, London EC2A 4LT. www.polyp@polyp.org.uk.

even further, to 1799 and the American President, Thomas Jefferson, who concluded that, 'Banking establishments are more dangerous than private armies.'[5]

If Brown had listened to these warnings, the government could have clamped down on the greed and incompetence of the bankers and financiers as they collected their millions in bonuses, salaries, bloated pension pots and pay offs. Brown could then have prevented many jobs from being lost, homes being re-possessed and our taxes raided of billions of pounds to support the bankers.

The irony is that Brown had to return to some of the ideas held in his socialist days by taking into public ownership one of the banks, Northern Rock, while part nationalising some others. But these are merely temporary measures and there is no doubt that the additional proposed controls of the banking and finance sector are merely words, gestures to placate an angry public; as soon as possible, the banks will be returned to private ownership. The harsh reality is that our future will once again be left to free market forces and an incompetent and immoral banking system.

Yet the bankers and financiers still appear on our television screens, demanding their 'efficiency' bonuses and expecting a gullible general public to accept their bad luck stories, as this Christmas card indicates.

Father Christmas against Fictitious Capital

KEEP IT REAL

Leeds Postcards; www.leedspostcards.com.

People were somewhat confused, after hearing the government's explanations of a shortage of money to finance socially useful projects, to suddenly witness the government handing out tens of billions of pounds to bail out the banks.

Another person Brown should have listened to was Karl Marx; as this Christmas card illustrates, he describes it as 'fictitious capital'. The card highlights that 'fictitious capital is that proportion of capital which cannot be simultaneously converted into existing use-values. It is an invention which is absolutely necessary for the growth of real capital; it constitutes the symbol of confidence in the future. It is a necessary but costly fiction, and sooner or later it crashes to earth.' That seems to sum up perfectly the present banking and financial crisis.

Yet Brown seemed to be abdicating any responsibility for this crisis, implying that it was just the result of international forces at work, which are beyond his control. He reminds me of another politician, Ramsey McDonald, the former Prime Minister and Labour Leader, who, when addressing his last Party Conference in 1930, declared 'Who does not know that the unemployment is of a totally different nature from that which we faced at the last general election. It has been caused by events, by forces and by movement common to the whole world.'[6]

Not surprisingly, *The Guardian* on-line Christmas cards for 2008 reflect the economic and banking crisis. The one of Gordon Brown has him delivering the words, 'And doona forget, kiddies, we'll be taking back all your presents next year.' This reflects that part of his policy to get us out of the crisis, of lowering taxes and spending more, while admitting, that it would all have to be paid back, with higher taxes and cuts in the near future.

This page: Artist: Martin Rowson; www.guardian.co.uk.

The Christmas card, featuring David Cameron, has him declaring, 'Please Sir, may we have less.' This is in response to his belief that the government is borrowing and spending too much.

The Guardian card featuring the Liberal Democrats, fails to refer to its leader, Nick Clegg; instead it shows their Treasury spokesperson, Vince Cable. He's shown saying: 'of course I predicted Christmas years ago,' which was a reminder that he had predicted the banking crisis.

Yet Brown did not just loyally serve the bankers and the financiers, but almost anyone who had 'loads of money'. If anyone should have doubted this, he announced the return of Peter Mandelson to the Cabinet. The man who found it acceptable for some to be 'filthy rich'.[7]

This fondness for the rich can also be seen in the limited response to the issue of tax havens, which Brown had chosen to ignore.

In contrast, Brown's treatment of those on the lower end of the wealth scale was not always generous, as shown by his 10p tax changes that would adversely affect the low paid. He was forced to introduce other changes to limit the damage of this policy. Lone parents, with children of one year of age or over, were also subject to sanctions if failing to prepare for employment and the planned use of lie detectors on benefit claimants. Yet in his more progressive anti-Thatcher days, when inequality was less than it is now, he still argued that 'The distribution of income in Britain has become so unequal that it is beginning to resemble a third world country.'[8] What was wrong then seemingly became acceptable.

The rich are also highlighted on the 'War on Want' Christmas cards, as they benefit from the slave labour conditions of many they indirectly employ for 5p an hour, 80 hours a week, in countries like Bangladesh, China, Honduras, to name but a few.

At the other end of the scale, the rich continued to demand more, while so many others were short of even basic necessities. Brown had shown that there was no shortage of money to support the banks. How could he be less generous when pleas were made for additional finances to support the essential services for the most vulnerable in our society?

If anyone still doubts that there was no shortage of money, then just remember that the money was found to go to war with Iraq and also increasingly with Afghanistan.

Brown announced the withdrawal of the majority of British troops from Iraq, but seemingly these forces were to be redeployed in Afghanistan for another worthless and bloody conflict. A card which reflected another aspect of the aftermath of the war in Iraq came in the form of a remark that on the twelfth day of Christmas, 2008, five British citizens had been held hostage for 576 days. Further cards were received, highlighting their continued captivity. Tragically, four of them were murdered by their captors. Although we have copies of these cards, we have not been able to make contact with the group, who had been campaigning for their release, and therefore we have been unable to obtain copyright permission to reproduce the cards here.

Still on the subject of the Middle East, Palestine increasingly resembles a prison, as the West Bank is surrounded by a 6-metre 'apartheid' wall. This tragedy increased as Israel bombarded other Palestinians in the Gaza with the most deadly conventional weapons, introducing the horrific 'white phosphorus' fire shells. It also invaded that land, killing over a thousand of its people, a third of these being children, while there were only a few Israeli military deaths and no Israeli civilian casualties.

Left: Artist: Lee O'Connor – Inbox@leeoconnor. com; War on Want; www.waronwant.org.

Below: Artist: Martin Rowson; www.guardian. co.uk.

Gathered Images.

The issue of global warming was taken up in a humorous way in one of the Christmas cards.

The planned expansion of Heathrow Airport would obviously have further damaged the environment and made worse the problems of climate change.

Another card reminds us of the continued support for the ban on hunting animals.

Now Martin Luther King had a 'Dream', so why shouldn't we? Liberty has one, as highlighted in their Christmas card. It's a good start but we are sure socialists would be willing to suggest a few additions.

While the words of Nelson Mandela remind us of how life should be.

On a different issue, another card demands 'Equal Rights for Agency Workers'.

'Liberty' continued their campaign via their Christmas card, urging us to be vigilant in the defence of our 'fundamental rights and freedoms' by referring to Articles 1-12 of the Human Rights Act.

The Christmas before the General Election brought a new set of cards, highlighting the possibility of a Cameron Tory government. One Christmas card already passed judgment on how his (dismissive) attitude to the poor would be.

Artist: Jim Medway, Leeds Postcards.

Watercolour by Christine Rainsford. Verse by Bryan Sobey and Christine Taylor.

Above left: League Against Cruel Sports, New Starling House, Holloway Hill, Godalming GU7 1QZ. www.league.org.uk.

Above right: Liberty & The Civil Liberties Trust; www.liberty-human-rights.org.uk.

Below: Designed by Helen Sartoris. Published by Paper Dove Co. Ltd.

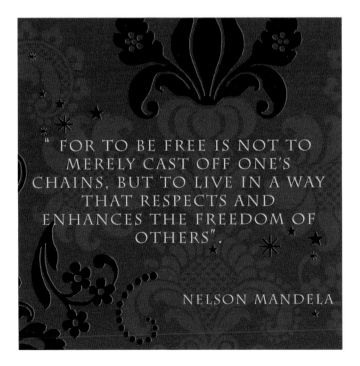

Above left: CWU, The Communications Union. www.cwu.org.

Above right: Liberty & the Civil Liberties Trust.

Left: Artist: Ian Hering, Leeds Postcards.

Above and below: Artist: Martin Rowson.

Artist: Julian Tudor Hart.

The bankers certainly were not in the mood to heed Gordon's advice, and as always with them, greed ruled.

In another, Brown is humorously portrayed trying to be all things to everyone with the words 'Hug a Herod'.

The final card in this chapter is a warning to 'Be Prepared for Anything in 2010!'

Notes on Chapter 13

1. Berthold Brecht, quoted in *Sound Bites*, New Internationalist Publications Ltd, Oxford, 1997.
2. George Orwell, *Animal Farm*, Penguin Books, 1968.
3. Digby Jones, speaking to a CBI Dinner in Glasgow, 3 September 2004.
4. John Maynard Keynes, quoted in *Moving Forward : Programme For a Participatory Economy* by Michael Albert, South End Press, Boston, USA, 2000.
5. Thomas Jefferson, quoted in *Tony Benn a Political Life* by David Powell, Continuum, London and New York, 2001.
6. Ramsay McDonald, quoted in *The Vote. How it was Won and how it was Undermined* by Paul Foot, Viking, 2005.
7. Peter Mandelson, *Financial Times*, 23 October 1998.
8. Gordon Brown, *Where there is Greed: Margaret Thatcher and the Betrayal of Britain's Future*, Mainstream Publishing, 1989.

CHAPTER 14

We Are Meant For Each Other

'Those who live in a palace do not think about the same things, nor in the same way, as those who live in a hut.'[1]

– Thomas Sankara

The Christmas card coinciding with Brown's final year in office warned us to 'Be Prepared for Anything in 2010' – how prophetic that was as we witnessed a not so typical British parliamentary coup with the Tories and the Liberal Democrats installing themselves in 10 Downing Street. With neither their decision to form a coalition government nor the policy programme they rolled out having been endorsed by the electorate, a coup seems a fair description of their actions; particularly when one considers that the majority of the programme was vastly different to what either one of the Coalition partners had campaigned for.

The naïve would not have expected the (so-called) Liberal Democrats to have been part of that shoddy Coalition, but as this Christmas card shows, Osborne and Cable are in bed together, while the cuts are being made.

In reality it was a coup by and for the rich. A coup led by multi-millionaires: Cameron, Clegg, Osborne and Hulme – unashamedly contemptuous of the feelings of the electorate, introducing the most right-wing agenda for the past century.

Yet we are expected to believe that the Coalition's programme is 'civilised'[2] – that is the opinion of Douglas Alexander, the Liberal Democratic Minister, who presumably is speaking on behalf of the Cabinet. If they should take a cursory glance at the dictionary definition of 'civilised' they would find that it includes the defining words '... refine, educate, or enlighten ...'[3] Not words that immediately come to mind when describing Coalition policies, made obvious in these Christmas cards.

The writer, Frank McKinney Hubbard argued that 'If the government was as afraid of disturbing the consumers, as it is of disturbing business, then this would be some democracy.'[4] While this applies to many governments, it does not apply to the present Coalition Government; they are in no danger of 'disturbing' business, the wealthy or the greedy, as they are a part of them, with an identical set of values.

With the Liberal Democrats in Government, seemingly determined to be as equally conservative as the Tories, the words of Connor Cruise O'Brien spring to mind: 'Liberalism ... made the rich world yawn and the poor world sick.'[5] Now it is probably more accurate to say that the rich world no longer yawns at the Liberals, but instead applauds them. Even Clegg recognised the contempt in which he was held by many, admitting that 'I'm so hated, people put dog mess through my door'.

Above left: www.proudtoservethepublic.org.uk.

Above right: Artist: Steve Smith.

Below: Artist: Martin Rowson.

Above: Artist: Polyp; Red Pepper. redpepper.org.uk.

Right: © George Blair 2010. george.blair.
uk@gmail.com.

Below: Printed and promoted by Nick Brown MP.

Above left: Morten Morland; adapted from the Smoking Gallery of the Reporters' Gallery, House of Commons, 1886 for the Parliamentary Press Gallery.

Above right: Artist: Gill Gough and John Plumpton for CND.

The Coalition's decision to ignore past promises and allow bankers to continue receiving their obscene bonuses is a classic, but not unexpected, example of defending their own class interests. While one Christmas card highlights the greed of the bankers, another sympathises with them, foolishly implying that Christmas will not be a happy one for bankers and he is glad that he is not one of them.

Among the financial crisis the voice of peace is still to be heard. CND continues to raise their voice for a saner world; if this should be heeded, then one of the many benefits would be savings of £100 billion with the cancellation of the successor to Trident, and fewer cuts in our public services as a result. Sadly, the Coalition is not listening. This card asks you to 'imagine' a world free from war and these weapons of mass destruction.

2011 witnessed the Trade Unions rising from their slumber and the birth of campaigning groups opposing corporate greed, unemployment, massive increases in student fees, cuts in public services, welfare benefits and, as a Christmas card highlights, pensions.

One of the groups, 'Occupy London', was even the subject of a letter from the police to the banking fraternity, headed 'Terrorism / Extremism' , warning that this group was

Above: Public and Commercial Services Union, 160 Falcon Road, London SW11 2LN.

Right: Artist: Diana Francis.

conducting 'hostile reconnaissance'[6] against them. Some of us thought that the real extremists (enemies) were the bankers but sadly the police and the establishment did not share that sentiment. The police, in their letter, went even further – grouping Occupy London with terrorist groups like Al-Qaida.[7] The attempts to liken perfectly legitimate groups to violent ones is reminiscent of the Thatcher era, when she described the miners as 'the enemy within'. Comparing her fight with them with the one against the Argentinean junta, following the Falklands War.[8]

Above: Produced by Liberty. Artist: Ian McDonald.

Below left: Labour Briefing; artist unknown.

Below right: Artist: Judy Horacek for Cath Tate Cards.

Cameron still declared that he supported the 'right to protest', while Clegg committed the Coalition 'to remove limits on the rights to peaceful protest',[9] yet failed to incorporate that sentiment in parliamentary legislation. Their support for the right to protest began and ended with certain countries in turmoil in the Middle East (sadly not Saudi Arabia). And certainly not against corporate greed in the City of London, a point made in one card. This became even more obvious when Cameron opposed what he described 'the right to erect tents all over the place',[10] which in reality meant on land owned by St Paul's Cathedral and his friends in the City of London. Sadly, even the church ignored their teaching by supporting the landowners, those guilty of corporate greed over the opponents of that greed.

None of the major parties in the UK are willing to tackle the bankers, who have blighted the lives of so many people. Why can't the Coalition legislate against the massive salaries and bonuses of bankers as they clamp down on low paid public service workers?

Another Christmas card concentrates on the crisis with the Euro and the increasing power of the European Central Bank, especially in countries where democratically elected governments have been replaced by unelected bankers, with joint policies forcing the people into destitution.

The failure of the Coalition to confront the bankers is similar to their refusal to tackle inequality. It would have been naïve to believe that a Cabinet full of multi-millionaires, committed to the values of capitalism, would wish to tackle inequality, benefiting those at the bottom of the pile. Similar hopes were expressed in one Christmas card, wanting an 'end to inequality', but with the response 'I think that'd have to be your birthday wish as well'.

Their response to unemployment and poverty is equally negative, as is their failure to tackle bankers and inequality. Do they share the belief that Thatcher espoused in the 1980s that today 'there is really no primary poverty left in this country ... there may be poverty because they don't know how to budget ... but now you are left with the really hard fundamental character / personality defect'[11]? I suspect this is so, as the Coalition's main aim seems to be to fight the poor and not poverty.

If the Coalition prioritised the unemployed and not the bankers, then the former could be a thing of the past. Just imagine if the Bank of England had used just £78 billion of the £325 billion of new money they created to bail out the bankers, then the 3 million unemployed could once again be gainfully employed based on an average annual income of £26,000.

Even the birds have no faith in the willingness of the Coalition Government to tackle unemployment as highlighted in a Christmas card with the slightly amended verse 'on the first day of Christmas, my Government gave to me an unemployed partridge on a downsized pear tree'. The bird's response was 'don't blame me – I didn't vote for them'.

Next year will surely include Christmas cards highlighting the Coalition's privatisation of the National Health Service, together with their decision to lower the tax rates for the richest while attacking the standard of living of the poorest.

In differing degrees, all the major political parties seem to share the Thatcher philosophy that there is no alternative to present policies. Compare their defeatism, their lack of an alternative vision with Clement Atlee, who, as Prime Minister, inherited a wrecked economy after the Second World War. In spite of that, he still created the jewel in our

Artist: Judy Horacek for Cath Tate Cards.

crown, the National Health Service, a massive house building programme, welfare reform to benefit us all, and transferred millions of soldiers into civilian employment. He showed that there was and is an alternative.

Yet we are still led to believe that we should not worry as Cameron and his Coalition partners claim to be opposed to 'crony capitalism' while Miliband supports 'responsible capitalism'. I suspect many of the characters portrayed in this history of protest Christmas cards would share the belief that capitalism and the class system are, by their very nature, based on 'cronyism'. 'Responsible' capitalism is the biggest of all contradictions and is no more than a dream; what they should demand is 'responsible socialism'.[12]

Notes on Chapter 14

1. Thomas Sankara quoted in *Sound Bites*, New Internationalist Publications, 1997.
2. Douglas Alexander, quoted in *The Guardian*, 29 December 2010.
3. *The Collins Concise*, published by Collins, 1988.
4. Frank McKinney Hubbard, quoted in *Sound Bites*, New Internationalist Publication, 1997.
5. Connor Cruise O'Brien, quoted in *The Guardian*, letter column, March 2012.
6. Quoted by George Monbiot, *The Guardian*, 10 January 2012.
7. Quoted by George Monbiot, *The Guardian*, 10 January 2012.
8. Quoted by Seumas Milne in *The Enemy Within*, published by Verso, 1994.
9. Quoted by George Monbiot, *The Guardian*, 10 January 2012.
10. Quoted by George Monbiot, *The Guardian*, 10 January 2012.
11. Quoted by Owen Jones, *Chavs – The Demonization of the Working Class*, published by Verso.
12. Peter Woodcock, quoted in *The Guardian*, letter column, 10 January 2012.

Conclusion

'Sometimes it seems that we have to keep fighting the same battles over and over. But every now and then, the mist does rise and we can see how far we have come.'[1]
— *Pete Seeger, 1986*

The writer, Selma James, once said that 'it's the business of politicians ... to keep the lid on ... and they do it in a variety of ways. They manage us. That's their job. That's all. They discourage us from going for the things we want. They offer cups of tea at crucial moments to prevent us from boiling over ...'[2]

David Rubenstein builds on the thoughts of both Seeger and James by not only pointing out how the establishment attempts to 'keep the lid on', but also how, on occasions, we manage to remove it. Firstly, the establishment declares that '... the demand is impossible; insist when it has proved to be popular, that the time for its translation into statute has not yet come ... when it is clear that there appears to be some urgency about it, insist that you cannot yield to violence ... [but] when you are driven to yield ... [say it is] because you have been intellectually convinced that the perspective of events have changed.'[3]

The establishment represented in recent years by parties with many similar policies – New Labour, the Tories and Liberal Democrats – has continually attempted to stifle protest to 'keep the lid on'. Anyone who is perceived to be a threat to their values must be stopped, as others have, from the Levellers to the Chartists and Suffragettes. Dissent is not acceptable.

The Christmas cards in this book almost invariably highlight these and many other obstacles, while reinforcing Pete Seeger's belief that while the struggle is often hard, with many setbacks, there are also victories. Many of them, while recognising these obstacles but refusing to take 'no' for an answer, 'keep the lid on', or accept that the 'demand is impossible'. But most seem determined to knock the 'lid off', recognising the importance of holding on to their hopes and thereby helping to ensure the victory does come, and the 'mist does rise'.

Often, when attempting to knock that lid off, the support of so-called important people is sought, like professional politicians and trade union leaders. Some respond positively and become an important part of the struggle. Yet the 'rebels', while recognising this, are still wise enough to also recognise that if such support is not forthcoming, then they have little option but to carry on without it. They then begin to learn, if they were not already aware, that their own power, when used collectively, can and often has knocked that lid off. The Christmas cards highlight many of these occasions, together with the failures, which are also reminders of how far we still have to travel. Either way, we must still educate, organise and hang on to our hopes, still proud to be socialists.

Notes on Conclusion

1. Pete Seeger, *Carry it On*, Blandford Press, Dorset, 1986.
2. Selma James.
3. David Rubenstein.

Artist: Maggie Guillon, devised by Trudy Begg.